Your Glorious Inheritance

You Can Access It Now!

SELLAPPAN PALANIAPPAN

ANISSA P. ZUCKER

Copyright © <2025> <Sellappan Palaniappan>

Made with ♥ on the Notion Press Platform

www.notionpress.com

Summary

Your Glorious Inheritance: You Can Access It Now! unveils the revolutionary truth about our inheritance in Christ as a present reality, not just a future promise. This book explores how we're included in divine life and called to manifest this inheritance now through understanding our true identity and position.

The journey begins with understanding the Trinity as the pattern for all life, showing how divine communion forms our inheritance's foundation. We discover our eternal selection in Christ before time began—not as an afterthought but as part of God's original design. This transforms our identity by revealing that God sees His own image within us. This divine life flows through His imperishable seed within us, carrying the complete pattern of divine nature, like a seed containing an entire forest's potential.

Through theosis—participation in divine nature—we become fully human by becoming divine, following the pattern of Israel's journey from slavery to sonship. As we break free from false identity and limiting beliefs, we're placed as mature sons, positioned to represent family interests. This relationship is unbreakable; we work with God as partners rather than servants, participating in divine creativity and purpose.

From this position of sonship, we naturally displace modern giants—religious mindsets, performance mentality, and false identity. Living from union becomes our natural way of being, with each person expressing divine glory uniquely through their personality and gifts, not through struggle but through awareness of who we are.

This manifestation extends beyond personal transformation to all creation, which eagerly awaits the revealing of mature sons. Our inheritance includes union with God, eternal life, divine wisdom, supernatural provision, and authority to impact creation. Through consciousness of our union with Christ, we naturally express divine nature, transforming both ourselves and creation around us.

The book concludes by showing how this understanding revolutionizes daily living. From family relationships to workplace challenges, from creative endeavors to world-changing initiatives, everything flows from our position as heirs of God and joint-heirs with Christ. This isn't just theology—it's practical reality available now to those who dare to live from their true identity in Christ. The central message remains: divine life isn't something to achieve but something to manifest from our existing union with God.

Acknowledgements

The completion of Your Glorious Inheritance: You Can Access It Now! has been a remarkable journey, and we are deeply grateful for the various sources of support, inspiration, and guidance that made this work possible.

First and foremost, we thank God for the revelation of His glorious inheritance, which has unfolded so beautifully throughout this book. Every word is a reflection of His eternal love and grace, and our prayer is that this book will help others see the majesty of His plan for all creation.

Special thanks go to The Passion Translation (TPT) for its fresh and deeply moving rendering of the Scriptures. The TPT's focus on the heart of God's love and grace has profoundly influenced the tone and direction of this book. Additionally, other Bible translations such as the Mirror Bible, New International Version (NIV), New Living Translation (NLT), and English Standard Version (ESV) provided crucial scriptural foundations, helping us present these truths with both clarity and theological integrity.

We are also grateful for the assistance of Claude, an advanced AI assistant, whose help with editing, refining ideas, and providing feedback proved invaluable throughout the writing process. While maintaining the authentic voice and message of the book, this technological tool helped bring greater clarity and coherence to the presentation of these eternal truths.

We want to acknowledge Tommy Miller, Chris Blackeby, Greg Lilley, Don Keithley, Damon Thompson, Mike Parsons, Jamie Englehart, Malcolm Smith, John Crowder, Baxter Kruger, Paul Young, Gil and Adena, Liz Wright, Phelim Doherty, Nanci Coen, Justin Abraham, and many others who have been very influential in shaping our understanding of our inheritance in Christ. Their teachings, writings, and ministries have deeply impacted our spiritual journey, and their insights have helped illuminate the profound truths of God's eternal purpose. We also extend our thanks to the wider community of scholars, theologians, and authors whose works have contributed to our understanding. Though many have not been referenced directly, their insights have shaped our thinking and fuelled our passion for sharing these glorious revelations.

Special thanks to Anna Teo for generously taking your precious time to review, provide feedback, edit, and proofread the manuscript multiple times. Your swift and excellent service is deeply appreciated. This manuscript could not have been completed without your willing and generous support, and labor of love.

Finally, to our readers—thank you for embarking on this journey with us. Our hope is that this book will stir your heart, challenge your understanding, and ultimately lead you deeper into the revelation of God's love and your identity in Him. It is for you, the seekers and disciples of Christ, that this work was written, and we pray it will encourage you to walk boldly into your destiny.

To God be the glory, now and forever.

About the Authors

Dr. Sellappan Palaniappan is a Professor of Information Technology at HELP University, Malaysia, with a Master's degree from the University of London (UK) and a PhD from the University of Pittsburgh (USA). He teaches Artificial Intelligence, Machine Learning, Data Science, and Cybersecurity, while maintaining interests in Quantum Physics, DNA, Neuroscience, Energy, Frequency Vibration, Healing, and Wholeness.

His ministry work includes serving as a Local Elder (15+ years), Editor and Contributor to a Christian magazine (10+ years), Prison Ministry Counsellor (10+ years), and sharing the Gospel with undergraduate students (10 years). Dr. Sellappan embraces Trinitarian, Incarnational, Christo-centric, Inclusive, and Grace theology, believing in God's goodness and Christ's finished work for all.

Anissa Zucker lives in New Hartford, Connecticut, with her husband David, daughter Melody, and their mini Goldendoodle, Mitzy. A devoted follower of Jesus, she helps others discern truth from lies and recognize God as the unconditionally loving Creator of all things.

Anissa works as a special education para-educator and advocates for neurodivergent individuals. She founded the Kainos Joy Podcast, sharing her ADHD journey and faith transformation. With a master's in literacy education, she has worked as a literacy consultant, ESL teacher, reading tutor, author, and illustrator, publishing children's books and poetry.

Balancing motherhood with her professional pursuits, Anissa engages with her daughter on academic and imaginative adventures while writing inspirational blog posts. Her calling is to empower neurodivergent individuals, share Christ's "finished work," and inspire others through her words and actions. She is a graduate of Cana New Wine and studies at Global Grace Seminary.

Table of Contents

Chapter 1   **The Divine Dance: Trinity as Pattern**   **14**
- The Eternal Dance of Love
- Divine Union and Distinction
- The Economy of Love and Its Flow
- Creation as Expression of Trinitarian Life
- Our Inclusion in Divine Family
- Practical Implications for Daily Life
- Living from Union: Patterns for Daily Practice
- Stories of Trinitarian Patterns in Action
- Transformation through Participation
- Chapter Summary
- Reflection Questions

Chapter 2   **Chosen in Christ Before Time**   **25**
- Our Pre-time Reality in Christ
- The Eternal Purpose
- Our Pre-existence in Christ
- Transcending Temporal Boundaries
- The Implications of Eternal Selection
- Living from Pre-time Reality
- Practical steps for living from this reality
- Chapter Summary
- Reflection Questions

Chapter 3   **The God Who Believes in Us**   **33**

- Divine Confidence in His Image
- Seeing through God's Eyes
- His Complete Confidence
- Beyond Human Assessment
- The Power of His Perspective
- Living from His Faith
- Practical steps for living from His faith
- Chapter Summary
- Reflection Questions

Chapter 4   **Divine Life Through Imperishable Seed**   **44**

- The Power of Imperishable Seed
- The Nature of Imperishable Seed
- Divine DNA in Action
- Full Pattern of Divine Life
- Manifesting the Seed's Potential
- Living from Divine Nature
- Practical steps for living from divine nature
- Chapter Summary
- Reflection Questions

Chapter 5   **The Mystery of Theosis**   **55**

- Transformation into Divine Nature
- The Divine-Human Reality
- Beyond Religious Effort
- Union and Distinction
- Manifesting Divine Nature
- Living in Theosis
- Practical steps for living in theosis

- Chapter Summary
- Reflection Questions

Chapter 6   **The Journey from Slavery to Sonship**   70
- Our Journey to Inheritance
- From Egypt to Freedom
- Wilderness Training
- Crossing Jordan
- Giants in the Land
- Living as Mature Sons
- Practical expressions of mature sonship
- Chapter Summary
- Reflection Questions

Chapter 7   **Breaking Free from False Identity**   83
- The Journey to Authentic Self
- Understanding False Identity
- The Two Sons' Delusion
- Recognizing the True Self
- Breaking Free from False Patterns
- Living from True Identity
- Practical expressions for daily life
- Chapter Summary
- Reflection Questions

Chapter 8   **Placement as Mature Sons**   98
- Beyond Traditional Adoption
- Understanding Huiothesia
- From Children to Mature Sons
- The Stages of Maturity
- The Position of Maturity
- Family Authority and Responsibility
- Living as Placed Sons

- Practical Expressions and Signs
- Chapter Summary
- Reflection Questions

Chapter 9   **Nothing Can Separate**   **111**
- Unbreakable Union
- Understanding Unbreakable Union
- Beyond Performance to Position
- Divine Love's Perfect Work
- Love That Never Fails
- Living from Eternal Security
- Manifesting Unbreakable Life
- Chapter Summary
- Reflection Questions

Chapter 10   **Working With God, Not for God**   **123**
- Partnership Over Performance
- The Language of Union
- From Service to Partnership
- Divine Collaboration
- Natural Co-Creation
- Family Business Model
- Living from Union
- Chapter Summary
- Reflection Questions

Chapter 11   **Displacing Modern Giants**   **134**
- Overcoming Present-Day Strongholds
- Modern Giants Identified
- The Seven Mindset Giants
- From Fear to Faith
- Position Over Performance
- Displacement Through Rest
- Living Above Giants

- Chapter Summary
- Reflection Questions

Chapter 12   Living from Union   **147**
- One Spirit Reality
- Our Heart-Brain Coherence
- Understanding One Spirit Reality
- Natural Expression of Union
- Daily Life in Union
- Union Consciousness
- Living as One
- Chapter Summary
- Reflection Questions

Chapter 13   Unique Glory Expression   **158**
- Individual Manifestation of Divine Life
- Hidden Glory Revealed
- Understanding Unique Design
- Glory Through Personality
- Individual Manifestation
- Corporate Harmony
- Living Your Glory
- Chapter Summary
- Reflection Questions

Chapter 14   Cosmic Restoration   **168**
- Creation Awaits Sons
- Understanding Cosmic Purpose
- Creation's Groaning
- Sons as Restorers
- The Scope of Restoration
- Manifesting Glory
- Living Restoration Now
- Chapter Summary
- Reflection Questions

Chapter 15   Present-Tense Inheritance   179
- Living from What's Already True
- Understanding Present Reality
- Living from Fullness
- Manifesting Inheritance
- Kingdom Economics
- Accessing Now
- Chapter Summary
- Reflection Questions

Chapter 16   The New Creation Race   190
- Beyond First Adam
- Breaking Adam's Boundaries
- New Species Reality
- Divine-Human Nature
- Future Glory Manifesting
- Living New Creation Now
- Chapter Summary
- Reflection Questions

Chapter 1

The Divine Dance: Trinity as Pattern

The Eternal Dance of Love

Before time began, there was a dance—a dance of perfect love, perfect giving, perfect unity. This eternal dance of Father, Son, and Holy Spirit forms the pattern of all creation, all inheritance, and all life. To understand our glorious inheritance, we must first glimpse this divine choreography.

This isn't three gods cooperating, but one God existing as eternal communion. The Hebrew word for one (echad) used in "Hear O Israel, the Lord our God, the Lord is one" (Deuteronomy 6:4) captures this reality—it's the same word used to describe how man and woman become "one flesh," suggesting a compound unity rather than solitary oneness.

The Passion Translation beautifully captures this eternal reality in John 1:1-2: "In the beginning the Living Expression was already there. And the Living Expression was with God, yet fully God. They were together—face-to-face, in the very beginning." This face-to-face communion reveals the intimate nature of God's eternal existence—a community of self-giving love.

Consider how Jesus describes this divine communion in John 17:21 (TPT): "I pray for them all to be joined together as one even as you and I, Father, are joined together as one. I pray for them to become one with us." This profound prayer reveals that the trinitarian pattern of union and communion was always meant to include us. We weren't created to merely observe the divine dance but to join it.

Divine Union and Distinction

The Trinity's eternal dance is characterized by mutual indwelling, or perichoresis as the early church fathers called it. In this divine choreography, each Person fully indwells the others while maintaining distinct identity. Jesus expressed this reality when He said, "The Father is in me and I am in the Father" (John 10:38 TPT). This mutual indwelling isn't just a theological concept—it's the blueprint for our inheritance.

Think of a perfect waltz where each dancer moves in complete harmony with the others, yet each maintains their distinctive role. The beauty comes not from uniformity but from unity—each participant enriching the dance through their unique contribution. Even in nature, we see this pattern: consider how a symphony creates harmony not by all instruments playing the same note, but by each contributing its unique voice to the whole.
Let me continue with the refined next sections:

The Economy of Love and Its Flow

The divine economy operates on an entirely different principle from human systems—one of perpetual giving rather than transaction or accumulation. Within the Trinity, we see an eternal cycle where each member constantly pours out to the others, creating an infinite flow of love and life. Like an endless river flowing in a perfect circle, this divine economy becomes our model for living.

Think about how radically different this is from human economics. In our world, resources are considered limited, leading to competition and scarcity thinking. But in the divine economy, giving multiplies abundance. The Mirror Bible captures this transformative reality in 2 Corinthians 9:8: "God is able to make every grace overflow toward you, so that in all things, at all times, having all that you need, you will overflow in every good work."

Jesus demonstrated this economy when He fed thousands with a few loaves and fish. The more the bread was broken and given, the more it multiplied. This wasn't just a miracle; it was a revelation of how trinitarian economy works—abundance flows through giving rather than hoarding. We see this pattern throughout creation: a single seed dies to produce countless new seeds; love multiplies through sharing; knowledge grows by being given away.

This eternal flow isn't just something to admire from afar—it's the very life we're invited into. When Paul writes in Romans 8:17 (TPT) that we are "joint heirs with Christ," he's declaring our inclusion in this divine economy of giving and receiving. The Father eternally loves the Son, the Son eternally loves the Spirit, the Spirit eternally loves the Father, in an unbroken circle of perfect communion that now includes us. As The Mirror Bible expresses in Romans 5:5, "And this hope is not a disappointing fantasy, because we can now experience the endless love of God cascading into our hearts through the Holy Spirit who lives in us!"

Creation as Expression of Trinitarian Life

Just as a master craftsman's work bears their signature, all creation bears the imprint of trinitarian life. The universe isn't just made by the Trinity; it's made like the Trinity, expressing in countless ways the pattern of divine communion. The Mirror Bible illuminates this reality in Romans 1:20: "For since the creation of the world His invisible attributes are clearly seen, being understood by the things that are made, even His eternal power and divine nature."

Look at the very structure of creation. At its most fundamental level, we find relationship and interconnection. Ecosystems thrive through intricate webs of giving and receiving—trees release oxygen that animals breathe; animals release carbon dioxide that plants need; the waste of one organism becomes food for another. Nothing exists in isolation; everything participates in a grand dance of mutual giving and receiving.

The Passion Translation renders Colossians 1:16-17: "For through him God created everything in the heavenly realms and on earth... all things were created through him and for him. He existed before anything else, and he holds all creation together." Christ doesn't just hold creation together externally—He holds it together through the same pattern of self-giving love that characterizes the Trinity.

Even human creativity reflects this pattern. When we're at our most creative, we're never truly creating alone. As beings made in God's image, our creativity flows from our participation in divine creativity. The Mirror Bible expresses this in Ephesians 2:10: "We are his poetry, created in Christ Jesus for good works which God prepared beforehand that we should walk in them."

Our Inclusion in Divine Family

There's a vast difference between visiting a family and being part of a family. A visitor might share a meal, enjoy conversation, even stay for a while—but family belongs. Family shares DNA, carries the name, inherits naturally. And here's the astounding truth—we're not visitors in God's house. We're family.

Jesus makes this breathtakingly clear in John 20:17 (TPT): "Stop clinging to me, for I haven't yet ascended to my Father. But go to my brothers and tell them that I am ascending to my Father and your Father, to my God and your God!" Notice how Jesus doesn't say "my Father and their Father" but "my Father and your Father." He's declaring our complete inclusion in His relationship with the Father.

This isn't adoption in the modern sense of bringing in someone from outside the family. The Greek word huiothesia, often translated as adoption, actually means "placement as sons." We weren't outsiders who God decided to adopt—we were family in His heart before creation began. The Mirror Bible illuminates this in Ephesians 1:5: "He pre-designed us to be his own children... This was his intent and pleasure."

Practical Implications for Daily Life

Truth that doesn't transform daily life remains merely theoretical. The reality of trinitarian life and our inclusion in it revolutionizes how we live every moment of every day. Consider how this understanding transforms our basic activities:

Morning Awakening: Instead of waking to an identity shaped by performance or problems, we wake to the reality that we're already included in Christ's perfect relationship with the Father. The Mirror Bible expresses this in 1 Corinthians 6:17: "The one joined to the Lord exists as one spirit with him!" You don't have to build a relationship with God today—you're already sharing His life.

Prayer: Prayer shifts from trying to bridge a gap between us and God to participating in Jesus' own communion with the Father. As The Mirror Bible captures in Romans 8:15-16: "The Spirit you received does not make you slaves, so that you live in fear again;

rather, you received the Spirit of sonship, by whom we cry, 'Abba, Father!'"

Work: We're not working for God as servants trying to please a distant master. We're working with God as family members expressing His creativity and love. Whether you're coding software, caring for children, building houses, or serving customers, you're participating in God's ongoing creative work.

Relationships: When we know we're included in the divine flow of giving and receiving, we naturally:
- Give freely because we're receiving constantly
- Love unconditionally because we're loved perfectly
- Forgive readily because we're forgiven completely
- Create boldly because we share divine creativity

A master artist captured this perfectly when teaching a struggling student: "Stop trying to create something impressive. Start recognizing the creativity already flowing through you. You're not the source—you're the channel. Your job isn't to generate creativity but to let it flow."

Living from Union: Patterns for Daily Practice

Living from our union with God transforms how we handle every situation. We're not facing challenges alone or in our own strength—we're experiencing them from within the circle of trinitarian life, where Christ's victory is our victory, His resources our resources, His peace our peace. The Mirror Bible expresses this in 2 Corinthians 1:20: "For all the promises of God in Him are Yes, and in Him Amen."

Consider these practical expressions:

When Facing Anxiety:
Rather than trying to generate peace, rest in Christ's own peace with the Father. Like a child naturally secure in their parents' love, you're held in the same love that holds the Trinity together.

In Decision-Making:
Instead of striving to figure everything out, access the wisdom already available through your union with Christ. Like a branch naturally drawing life from the vine, let wisdom flow from connection rather than mental effort.

In Challenging Relationships:
You're participating in God's own capacity to love. Rather than trying to manufacture love from your own resources, let it flow from His abundance. Like a river flowing from a full reservoir, divine love moves naturally through you.

During Intensive Work:
You're joining God's creative activity, not performing for Him. Like a musician in perfect flow with the music, let divine energy express through you rather than pushing from your own strength.

When Facing Setbacks:
Remember your identity isn't in your performance but in your inclusion in Christ. Like a child secure in family belonging regardless of achievement, nothing can separate you from this love.

A business executive discovered this reality when overwhelmed with responsibilities. She shifted from trying to generate wisdom for each decision to tapping into divine wisdom already available through her union with Christ. Her decision-making transformed from pressure to flow, from striving to receiving.

Stories of Trinitarian Patterns in Action

Sometimes abstract truths become clearest through real-life manifestations. Here are living examples of how trinitarian patterns transform everyday situations:

The Artist's Discovery:
Sarah spent years believing she had to choose between her art and her faith, seeing them as separate realms. While meditating on Colossians 1:16—"For through him God created everything"—

she realized her creativity wasn't separate from God's but participation in it. Her studio became a sanctuary where divine life flows through her unique artistic expression, like the Trinity's eternal creative expression.

The Community Transformation:
The Martinez family revolutionized their neighborhood by living from trinitarian patterns. Instead of viewing their home as a private refuge, they reimagined it as a hub of giving and receiving. Their garage became a shared workshop, their dining room a gathering place for community meals, their garden a collaborative project. The Mirror Bible captures the fruit of their transformation in Acts 2:46-47: "They shared life together with uncluttered hearts... and daily more and more people were added to their number."

The Business Renewal:
James restructured his company around mutual giving—between employees, with customers, and toward the community. He implemented profit-sharing, mentoring programs, and community service initiatives. His business became a living picture of the divine economy where giving multiplies resources rather than depleting them.

The Multicultural Symphony:
A local church discovered how to reflect trinitarian unity-in-diversity. Like the Trinity, where each Person is distinct yet perfectly one, this community learned to celebrate their differences while maintaining deep unity. African, Asian, European, and Latino expressions of worship flowed together in a tapestry of praise, demonstrating how distinct voices create richer harmony.

Transformation through Participation

In the end, transformation isn't about trying harder or doing better—it's about awakening to the reality that we're already included in the divine dance. The Mirror Bible expresses this in 2 Corinthians 3:18: "In him, every face mirrors the glory of the

Lord. We are transfigured by the Spirit of the Lord in our constant beholding, from glory to glory."

This transformation happens not through imitation but participation. Like learning to dance, you can study steps intellectually, but real dancing happens only when you let the music move through you, when you become one with the rhythm. Similarly, authentic Christian life isn't about memorizing rules or copying behaviors—it's about letting the divine dance move through us.

The Passion Translation captures this beautifully in Galatians 2:20: "My old identity has been co-crucified with Messiah and no longer lives. The essence of this new life is no longer mine, for the Anointed One lives his life through me—we live in union as one!"

This participation transforms everything because it works from the inside out:

- We're not trying to reach God—we're living from our inclusion in God's life
- We're not working for love—we're working from love
- We're not striving for acceptance—we're living from acceptance

Like a vine expressing its life through branches, the trinitarian pattern of self-giving love becomes our natural way of being. Just as a child naturally reflects their parents' mannerisms simply by living in close relationship, we begin to reflect the trinitarian pattern of love by living in conscious awareness of our inclusion in divine life.

This transformation extends beyond personal benefit—we become conduits of divine love, extending the dance to include others. The circle of giving and receiving that characterizes the Trinity begins to flow through our relationships, work, and creative expressions. We become living invitations to others to join the dance.

Chapter Summary

Our glorious inheritance flows from and reflects the eternal dance of trinitarian love. We were created for inclusion in this divine life, designed to participate in the perfect giving and receiving that characterizes God's eternal existence. This isn't just a beautiful theory—it's the fundamental pattern of reality itself. When we understand this trinitarian foundation, it transforms everything: we see God not as a solitary ruler but as eternal communion of love; we view ourselves not as servants trying to please God but as children sharing His life; we recognize creation not as separate from God but as expressing His nature; we approach relationships not as transactions but as opportunities for giving and receiving love; and we live not through effort but through participation in divine life. Like a perfect dance where each partner moves in harmony with the others, we find our place in the eternal choreography of trinitarian love, expressing and experiencing the fullness of our inheritance through conscious participation in this divine communion.

Reflection Questions

1. How has your understanding of the Trinity shifted from seeing it as a theological puzzle to recognizing it as the pattern for all life?

2. In what areas of your life do you still operate from effort rather than participation in divine life?

3. How might your relationships transform if you lived consistently from the trinitarian pattern of self-giving love?

4. What would change in your daily activities if you approached them as participation in divine creativity rather than human effort?

5. Where do you see opportunities to extend the divine dance to others, inviting them into this circle of giving and receiving love?

Chapter 2

Chosen in Christ Before Time

Our Pre-Time Reality in Christ

In quantum physics, particles that once interacted remain eternally connected, regardless of time or distance. This scientific wonder offers a glimpse into a far greater reality—our eternal selection in Christ before time began. Like these entangled particles, we share an eternal connection with God that predates creation itself.

Before the first ray of light pierced the darkness, before the first star burst into brilliance—you existed in God's heart. Not as a possibility, not as a potential, but as a reality held in Christ. The Passion Translation captures this stunning reality in Ephesians 1:4-5: "Even before he made the world, he loved us and chose us in Christ to be holy and without fault in his eyes. God decided in advance to adopt us into his own family by bringing us to himself through Jesus Christ."

Notice the sequence: before creation came choosing. Before earth's foundation came divine selection. This isn't about God looking down the corridors of time to see who would choose Him—it's about God choosing us in Christ before time existed. The Mirror Bible expresses this in 2 Timothy 1:9: "His grace concluded our salvation before time began! We were known and named in Christ before the ages began!"

This eternal choosing changes everything about how we understand ourselves and our purpose. We didn't start when we were conceived—we started in God's heart before creation began. Our identity isn't primarily shaped by our choices or circumstances—it's established in God's pre-time selection of us in Christ.

The Eternal Purpose

When we speak of purpose, we often think in terms of discovering it, as if it's something we need to find or achieve. But what if purpose isn't something we discover but something we've been chosen for from eternity? The Passion Translation illuminates this reality in Ephesians 3:11-12: "This perfectly wise plan was destined from eternal ages and fulfilled completely in our Lord Jesus Christ."

This eternal purpose centers on family. As The Mirror Bible captures, "He pre-designed us to be his own children. This was his intent and pleasure." The purpose wasn't merely to save us from something but to include us in Someone—to make us participants in the very life of God.

Think about how a master architect designs a building. Every detail is planned before construction begins—every room, every window serves a purpose in the overall design. Similarly, your place in God's family wasn't an adaptation to circumstances but part of the original blueprint. You weren't added to the plans later—you were in the plans before the foundation was laid.

The Passion Translation expresses this pre-time purpose in 2 Timothy 1:9-10: "Before times eternal he planned our glory: For he chose us and called us to this holy calling, not because of any good works we had done, but because of his own plan and grace given to us in the Messiah Jesus before time began!"

This eternal purpose reveals something profound about God's nature. He didn't wait to see how things would turn out before deciding to include us. He didn't react to our need—He acted from His love. The Fall didn't surprise Him or require a Plan B. His eternal purpose of including us in His family life was Plan A, and it has never changed.

Our Pre-existence in Christ

When David declared in Psalm 139, "Your eyes saw my unformed substance," he was glimpsing a reality that extends far beyond physical conception. The Mirror Bible powerfully renders it: "Like an open book, you watched me grow from conception to birth; all the stages of my life were spread out before you, the days of my life all prepared before I'd even lived one day." Our existence in God's heart predates our existence in time and space.

This isn't mere foreknowledge—it's pre-existence in Christ. The Mirror Bible illuminates this in Ephesians 1:4: "He associated us in Christ before the fall of the world! Jesus is God's mind made up about us!" Think of how a symphony exists in the composer's mind before it's ever played. Every note, every harmony exists as a reality in the composer's consciousness before the first sound is heard.

This pattern of pre-time selection echoes through scripture. The Passion Translation captures Paul's realization in Galatians 1:15: "But God had chosen me and set me apart for his divine purpose before I was born." Just as an oak tree exists completely in its acorn before any roots appear, our entire existence was complete in Christ before any temporal manifestation.

This pre-existence isn't a theological abstraction—it's the foundation of our identity and security. We existed in Christ before we existed in Adam. Our inclusion in Christ's life predates our inclusion in Adam's fall. This is why Paul can say that we were crucified with Christ, buried with Him, raised with Him—because our union with Christ preceded our earthly existence.

Transcending Temporal Boundaries

Most of us think of our lives as bound by time—with a clear beginning at birth and stretching forward into an endless future.

But scripture reveals a more profound reality: our existence transcends time itself. We're not just eternal beings moving forward; we're eternal beings who were already included in Christ's eternal life before time began.

The Implications of Eternal Selection

Understanding our eternal selection in Christ revolutionizes every aspect of our existence. The Mirror Bible expresses this transformative truth in Ephesians 1:11: "In him we were also chosen, having been predetermined according to the plan of him who works out everything in conformity with the design of his will."

This eternal selection transforms:

Our Identity: We're not trying to become something—we're awakening to who we've always been in Christ. The Passion Translation captures this in 1 Peter 2:9: "But you are God's chosen treasure—priests who are kings, a spiritual 'nation' set apart as God's devoted ones."

Our Struggles: They're not defining moments—they're temporary distortions of an eternal reality. As the Mirror Bible illuminates in Romans 8:33-34: "Do you really think anyone could succeed to bring a charge against God's chosen ones? God himself has declared them innocent!"

Our Growth: We're not trying to attain something new; we're growing in awareness of what's eternally true. As 2 Peter 1:3 declares: "Everything we could ever need for life and complete devotion to God has already been deposited in us by his divine power."

Our Purpose: We're not searching for our purpose—we're awakening to the purpose we were chosen for before time began. The Mirror Bible captures this in Ephesians 2:10: "We are his poetry, we are the words of his story; we were created in Christ Jesus to give expression to his intent."

This eternal selection even transforms how we view time itself. Rather than seeing time as the container of our existence, we see it as the stage where eternal reality manifests. The Mirror Bible expresses this in 2 Corinthians 4:18: "We do not focus on what is seen but on what is unseen, since what is seen is temporary, but what is unseen is eternal."

Living from Pre-time Reality

How do we practically live from the reality of our eternal selection in Christ? The Mirror Bible points the way in Colossians 3:1-3: "If you are then risen with Christ, desire and pursue the things of the superior realm where Christ is seated at the right hand of God. Base your thoughts on the superior realm, not on the inferior realm of the earthly experience."

This reality transforms:

Our Prayer Life: Instead of praying to a distant God, we pray from our inclusion in Christ's perfect communion with the Father. The Spirit witnesses with our spirit that we are God's children.

Our Daily Decisions: We're not asking, "What would Jesus do?" as if He's a distant example. Instead, we're asking, "What is Christ, who lives in me, doing?" The Mirror Bible expresses this in Galatians 2:20: "I am crucified with Christ: nevertheless I live; yet not I, but Christ lives in me."

Our Challenges: Consider how differently a person approaches challenges when they know they've already been accepted into medical school versus someone still trying to gain acceptance. The first person studies from security, the second from anxiety. Similarly, we face every situation not from anxiety about the outcome but from the security of what's already true.

Our Relationships: We no longer relate to others based on their temporal appearance or behavior, but from our shared eternal inclusion in Christ. As 2 Corinthians 5:16-17 says: "Therefore, from now on, we regard no one according to the flesh... Therefore, if anyone is in Christ, he is a new creation."

Practical Steps for Living from this Reality

1. Begin each day by acknowledging your eternal position in Christ before engaging with circumstances.

2. When facing decisions, pause to remember that you're not working toward wisdom but living from the wisdom that's already yours in Christ.

3. In relationships, practice seeing others through the lens of their eternal selection rather than their temporal behavior.

4. Let your work flow from your eternal identity rather than trying to build an identity through your work.

Chapter Summary

Our eternal selection in Christ isn't just a theological concept—it's the foundation for transformed living. We were chosen in Christ before time began, included in His life before creation, and our existence transcends temporal boundaries. This reality transforms everything: our identity, our relationship with God, our approach to challenges, our interactions with others, and our entire way of being. We're not working toward something; we're living from an eternal reality that's already true in Christ. Like a tree whose roots reach deep into eternal soil, our life flows from this timeless selection and inclusion in divine life. This understanding revolutionizes how we see ourselves—not as separated beings trying to connect with God, but as eternally included sons and daughters discovering what has always been true. God's choice of us wasn't an afterthought or response to human failure; it was His original intent, woven into the fabric of creation itself. This consciousness of our eternal selection naturally displaces insecurity, fear, and performance mentality, replacing them with the unshakeable awareness of our belonging in God.

Reflection Questions

1. How does knowing you were chosen in Christ before time began change how you view your current circumstances?

2. What would change in your daily life if you consistently lived from the reality of your eternal selection?

3. How might your relationships transform if you viewed others through the lens of their eternal selection in Christ?

4. In what areas of your life do you find it most challenging to live from this pre-time reality?

5. What practical steps can you take to more fully align your daily experience with your eternal position in Christ?

Chapter 3

The God Who Believes in Us

Divine Confidence in His Image

We often speak of our faith in God, but have you ever considered God's faith in you? It might seem startling at first—the idea that the Creator of the universe believes in His creation. Yet this profound truth lies at the heart of our inheritance: God has complete faith in His own image and likeness within us.

The Mirror Bible captures this revolutionary perspective in Genesis 1:26-27: "God said, Let us make man in our image and in our likeness... God created man in his image and likeness; male and female he created them in his image." Notice the intentionality here—God wasn't experimenting or hoping for the best. He was expressing complete confidence in His own nature being reflected in humanity.

The Passion Translation illuminates this divine confidence in Psalm 139:13-14: "You formed my innermost being, shaping my delicate inside and my intricate outside, and wove them all together in my mother's womb. I thank you, God, for making me so mysteriously complex! Everything you do is marvelously breathtaking. It simply amazes me to think about it!" This isn't just poetic language—it's a declaration of God's absolute faith in His workmanship.

Think about it: God sees His own image in you. Like an artist who knows the masterpiece exists within the marble before the first chisel stroke, God sees His nature within you before it's fully manifest. The Mirror Bible expresses this beautifully in 2 Corinthians 3:18: "In him, every face mirrors the glory of the Lord. We are transfigured by the Spirit of the Lord in our constant beholding, from glory to glory; the image is restored in our thoughts according to the Original."

Think about it: God sees His own image in you. Consider how a diamond forms deep within the earth. Under intense pressure and heat, carbon atoms align perfectly with their true nature. Similarly, when we align with God's vision of us, we manifest the glory He already sees. Like the diamond, we're not becoming something foreign to our nature—we're manifesting what was always there.

We are, as scripture declares in Isaiah 51:1-2, 'hewn from the Rock.' The Mirror Bible illuminates this profound reality: 'Listen to me, you who follow after righteousness, you who seek the Lord: Look to the rock from which you were hewn.' This isn't mere poetic language—it speaks of our intrinsic nature, being of the same substance as our source. Just as Eve was taken from Adam's substance, we are taken from Christ's very life. We're not merely shaped by God externally; we're formed from His very nature.

Yet this truth often lies hidden beneath layers of veils—accumulated mindsets, false beliefs, and distorted self-images that obscure our true nature. Like a masterpiece covered by years of dust and grime, our true identity in Christ awaits unveiling. The Mirror Bible expresses this transformative process in 2 Corinthians 3:18: 'We all, with unveiled face, beholding as in a mirror the glory of the Lord, are being transformed into the same image from glory to glory.'

This unveiling isn't about becoming something new but about revealing what's already true. It's metanoia—a complete renovation of thought patterns until we see Christ unveiled in us. Each layer of false identity peeled away reveals more of our true nature in Him. The Passion Translation captures this in 2 Corinthians 3:16: 'But the moment one turns to the Lord with an open heart, the veil is lifted and they see.'"

This truth changes everything about how we understand our relationship with God. We're not trying to convince God to believe in us—He already has complete faith in His own nature within us. The question isn't whether God believes in us; the question is whether we'll align with His vision of who we truly are.

Seeing through God's Eyes

What does God see when He looks at you? Not your mistakes, not your struggles, not your past—He sees His own image and likeness. The Mirror Bible expresses this profound reality in 2 Corinthians 5:16-17: "Therefore, from now on, we regard no one according to the flesh... for anyone in Christ is a new creation! The old has gone, and in him all things have become new!" God sees you according to His eternal perspective, not according to temporal appearances.

Think of how a parent sees their child. Even when the child is struggling or making mistakes, the parent sees their own likeness, their own DNA, their own nature within that child. How much more does our heavenly Father see His own divine nature within us! The Passion Translation captures this beautifully in 1 John 3:1-2: "Look with wonder at the depth of the Father's marvelous love that he has lavished on us! He has called us and made us his very own children... Beloved, we are God's children right now; however, it is not yet apparent what we will become. But we do know that when it is finally made visible, we will be just like him, for we will see him as he truly is."

This divine perspective isn't wishful thinking—it's based on the reality of His imperishable seed within us. The Mirror Bible illuminates this in 1 Peter 1:23: "You are born again not from a seed that can perish, but from an imperishable seed, through the living and enduring word of God." God sees His own seed, His own nature, His own life within us, and He has complete faith in what that seed will produce.

Consider how Jesus saw people. When He looked at Simon, He saw Peter—the rock. When He looked at Saul the persecutor, He saw Paul the apostle. When He looked at a tax collector, He saw a disciple. The Passion Translation expresses this transformative vision in 2 Corinthians 5:16: "We view no one from a merely human point of view. Though we once viewed Christ that way, we no longer view him with limited human insight."

God's vision of us isn't based on our performance or potential—it's based on His own nature within us. The Mirror Bible renders Colossians 1:27: "The secret is simply this: Christ in you! He is your hope of glory!" When God looks at you, He sees Christ. Not as a distant goal to achieve, but as a present reality to manifest. This divine perspective even transcends our own self-perception. Many of us are like Gideon, seeing ourselves as the least in our father's house, while God addresses us as mighty warriors. The Mirror Bible captures this reality in Judges 6:12: "The angel of the Lord appeared to him and said, 'The Lord is with you, mighty warrior.'" God wasn't trying to encourage Gideon—He was declaring what He saw to be true about him.

His Complete Confidence

We often think of faith as something we need to generate toward God. But what if the deeper reality is that God has complete faith in His own nature within us? The Mirror Bible expresses this profound truth in 2 Timothy 2:13: "Even when we are faithless, he remains faithful; he cannot deny himself." God's confidence isn't based on our performance—it's based on His own nature, His own image, His own life within us.

Think about how a master craftsman has complete confidence in their work. They know exactly what materials they used, exactly how they fashioned each piece, exactly what the finished product will be. The Passion Translation captures this reality in Ephesians 2:10: "We have become his poetry, a re-created people that will fulfill the destiny he has given each of us, for we are joined to

Jesus, the Anointed One." God has absolute confidence in His craftsmanship because He knows exactly what He put within us.

This divine confidence goes beyond mere optimism. The Mirror Bible illuminates this in Philippians 1:6: "I am convinced that the same one who initiated this glorious expression in you will bring it to a perfect conclusion." God isn't hoping for the best—He's working with absolute certainty because He's working with His own nature, His own life, His own seed within us.

Consider how Jesus demonstrated this divine confidence. When He looked at Peter sinking in the waves, He saw the rock upon which He would build His church. When He looked at Thomas doubting, He saw the apostle who would proclaim His lordship. The Passion Translation expresses this confidence in John 1:42: "Jesus gazed upon him and said, 'You are Simon, son of John, but your new name will be Peter, the Rock.'" Jesus wasn't trying to motivate Peter—He was declaring with divine confidence what He knew to be true.

This complete confidence extends even to our failures and struggles. The Mirror Bible renders Romans 8:28: "Meanwhile we know that the love of God causes everything to mutually contribute to our advantage." God's confidence isn't shaken by our stumbles because He knows His own nature will prevail. Like a master chess player who can use every move, even apparent mistakes, to achieve victory, God works everything together according to His purpose because He has complete confidence in His own ability to bring about His desired end.

The implications are staggering. The Mirror Bible captures this in 1 John 4:17: "The same love that he is, we are in this world!" God has such complete confidence in His own nature within us that He declares us to be, in this world, the same love that He is. Not striving to become love, not trying to manifest love, but being the same love that He is.

Beyond Human Assessment

Human evaluation always falls short of divine perspective. We assess based on appearance, performance, and past experience. But God sees from an eternal perspective, looking at His own image within us. The Mirror Bible expresses this profound difference in 1 Samuel 16:7: "The Lord does not look at the things people look at. People look at the outward appearance, but the Lord looks at the heart." And what does He see in the heart? His own nature, His own life, His own seed.

Consider how radically different this is from our typical self-assessment. We often measure ourselves by our accomplishments, our failures, our comparison with others. But The Passion Translation reveals God's perspective in 2 Corinthians 10:12: "We dare not compare ourselves with those who commend themselves. They are not wise when they measure themselves by themselves and compare themselves with themselves." God's assessment transcends all human comparisons because He's looking at something humans can't see—His own nature within us.

Even our most mature spiritual evaluation falls short of God's perspective. The Mirror Bible illuminates this in 1 Corinthians 4:3-4: "I do not even judge myself... it is the Lord who judges me." Paul understood that even his own self-assessment wasn't the final word—God's perspective transcends all human judgment, including our own.

This truth transforms how we view our spiritual journey. We often assess our growth by comparing today with yesterday, measuring our progress against various standards. But The Passion Translation captures a different reality in 2 Corinthians 3:18: "We can all draw close to him with the veil removed from our faces. And with no veil we all become like mirrors who brightly reflect the glory of the Lord Jesus." God sees the unveiled glory that's already there, waiting to be manifested.

Think about how a master gardener looks at a seed. While others might see just a small, seemingly insignificant speck, the gardener sees the full-grown plant within it. They know exactly what that seed contains and what it will produce. The Mirror Bible expresses this reality in 1 John 3:9: "Those born of God carry his DNA; his seed remains permanently within them." God sees His own seed within us and knows exactly what it contains and what it will produce.

This divine assessment even transcends time itself. The Mirror Bible renders Romans 8:30: "He pre-designed us from the start to be modeled after the image of his Son... He sees us as already glorified." Notice the present tense of that last phrase—He sees us as already glorified. Not working toward glory, not hoping for glory, but already glorified because He sees His own glory within us.

The Power of His Perspective

When we begin to see ourselves as God sees us, everything changes. The Mirror Bible captures this transformative power in 2 Corinthians 3:18: "As the Spirit of the Lord works within us, we become more and more like him and reflect his glory even more." This transformation doesn't happen through our efforts to improve ourselves—it happens as we align with God's perspective of who we already are in Him.

Consider how Jesus' perspective transformed people. When He called Zacchaeus down from the tree, addressing him as a son of Abraham rather than a tax collector, that perspective transformed Zacchaeus instantly. The Passion Translation expresses this power in Luke 19:9: "Jesus said to him, 'Today salvation has come to this home, for this man too is a son of Abraham!'" Jesus' perspective didn't just describe reality—it released people into that reality.

Consider the parable of the merchant who sold everything to buy the field containing hidden treasure (Matthew 13:44). While traditionally seen as us finding Christ, there's a deeper reality: we are the treasure, and God sees Himself hidden within us. The Mirror Bible expresses this dual reality in 2 Corinthians 4:7: 'We have this treasure in earthen vessels, that the excellence of the power may be of God and not of us.' Just as an archaeologist sees a priceless artifact beneath layers of sediment while others see only dirt, God sees His own glory beneath our temporal circumstances. He is the treasure in us, and we are the treasure in Him. Like a master artist who sees their masterpiece hidden in raw marble, God sees His own image, His own nature, His own life hidden within our earthen vessels.

This explains God's complete faith in us—He's not betting on our human potential; He's investing in His own image hidden within us. He knows exactly what He placed there, exactly what He hid within these earthen vessels. The Passion Translation captures this in Colossians 1:27: 'Christ in you, the hope of glory!'"

This same transformative power is available to us today. The Mirror Bible illuminates this in Colossians 3:3-4: "Your life is now hidden with Christ in God. Christ is your life!" As we begin to see ourselves through God's eyes—as those who are hidden with Christ in God, as those whose very life is Christ—we naturally begin to manifest that reality. It's not about trying harder; it's about seeing clearer.

Think about how a butterfly emerges from its chrysalis. The butterfly doesn't try to become something new—it awakens to what it already is. The Mirror Bible expresses this reality in 2 Corinthians 5:17: "In Christ, every person discovers their true identity! The old is gone; look—what has become new is of the essence of God!" God's perspective of us isn't about what we should become; it's about who we already are in Christ.

This divine perspective has creative power. The Passion Translation renders Romans 4:17: "God calls things that don't exist as though they do exist." When God looks at us, He's not seeing wishfully—He's seeing creatively. His perspective carries the power to manifest what He sees. Just as He spoke light into existence by seeing it first, He speaks our true identity into manifestation by seeing it first.

Even our struggles take on new meaning when seen through God's eyes. The Mirror Bible captures this in 2 Corinthians 4:17: "Our momentary light affliction is far outweighed by the most amazing eternal weight of glory that is about to be unveiled within us." From God's perspective, our challenges aren't obstacles to overcome—they're opportunities for His glory to be revealed through us.

Living from His Faith

What would change if we lived each day from God's faith in us rather than our faith in Him? The Mirror Bible expresses this revolutionary shift in Galatians 2:20: "I am crucified with Christ: nevertheless I live; yet not I, but Christ lives in me: and the life which I now live in the flesh I live by the faith of the Son of God, who loved me, and gave himself for me." Notice carefully—we live by the faith OF the Son of God, not just faith IN the Son of God.

This isn't about mustering up more faith or trying harder to believe. It's about resting in His faith, His confidence, His absolute certainty about who we are. The Passion Translation illuminates this in Hebrews 12:2: "We look away from the natural realm and we focus our attention and expectation onto Jesus who birthed faith within us and who leads us forward into faith's perfection." Our faith isn't something we generate—it's His faith being expressed through us.

Consider how this transforms our daily life. When we wake up in the morning, instead of trying to face the day in our own strength and confidence, we can rest in His complete faith in His nature within us. The Mirror Bible captures this reality in 1 John 4:17: "The same love that he is, we are in this world!" We're not trying to become love—we're resting in the fact that we already are the same love He is.

This shifts everything about how we approach challenges. Instead of wondering if we have enough faith to overcome, we can rest in

His faith in us. The Mirror Bible renders Romans 8:37: "In all these things we are super conquerors through him who loved us!" We're not trying to become conquerors—we're living from His faith that we already are super conquerors through His love.

Practical Steps for Living from His Faith

Begin each day by acknowledging His complete confidence in you. Before you face any challenges or tasks, remind yourself that God has absolute faith in His own nature within you. The Mirror Bible expresses this in Philippians 1:6: "I am convinced that the same one who initiated this glorious expression in you will bring it to a perfect conclusion."

When doubts arise, remember that His faith in you is greater than your doubts about yourself. The Passion Translation captures this in 2 Timothy 2:13: "Even when we are faithless, he remains faithful, for he cannot deny himself." His faithfulness isn't dependent on your faith—it's rooted in His own nature.
In relationships, practice seeing others through His eyes of faith. Just as He sees His nature in you, He sees it in them. This transforms how we interact with everyone we meet. The Mirror Bible guides us: "From now on we recognize no one according to their actions or appearance."

When facing decisions, rest in His wisdom within you rather than striving to figure everything out. The Mirror Bible expresses this in 1 Corinthians 2:16: "We have the mind of Christ!" You're not trying to access His wisdom—you're living from it.

Let your work flow from His confidence in you rather than your confidence in yourself. The Passion Translation renders Philippians 2:13: "God himself is at work in you, inspiring you to want those things which please him and to work for them."

Chapter Summary

God's faith in us precedes and transcends our faith in Him. He sees His own image, His own nature, His own life within us, and He has complete confidence in what He has placed there. This isn't wishful thinking—it's based on the reality of His imperishable seed within us. As we learn to live from His faith in us rather than our faith in Him, we begin to manifest naturally what He sees consistently. We're not trying to become something new; we're awakening to who we've always been in His sight. Like an acorn carrying the full potential of an oak tree, His imperishable seed within us contains everything necessary for divine expression. This transforms our entire approach to spiritual growth—instead of striving to develop faith in God, we're learning to rest in and live from His unwavering faith in us. His confidence in what He has planted within us becomes the foundation for our own confidence and expression of divine life.

Reflection Questions

1. How does understanding God's complete faith in you change how you view your challenges?

2. What would change in your relationships if you consistently saw others through God's eyes of faith?

3. How might your approach to spiritual growth shift if you lived from His faith in you rather than your faith in Him?

4. What areas of your life most need to be seen through His perspective?

5. How can you practically begin to live more consistently from His faith in you?

Chapter 4

Divine Life Through Imperishable Seed

The Power of Imperishable Seed

Consider this remarkable discovery: seeds found in ancient Egyptian pyramids, after lying dormant for thousands of years, still maintained their capacity to sprout and produce life when planted. If natural seeds can preserve their life-giving potential through millennia, how much more does God's imperishable seed within us maintain its divine potential! The Mirror Bible expresses this reality in 1 Peter 1:23: 'You have been born again, not of perishable seed, but of imperishable, through the living and enduring word of God.'

This truth brings hope to those who feel they've lost years to darkness or dormancy. Like those ancient seeds suddenly exposed to the right conditions, the divine seed within you hasn't lost any of its potential through time or circumstance. Whether you've been in your own 'pyramid' of isolation, imprisonment, or spiritual dormancy for years or decades, God's seed remains fully potent, ready to produce divine life. The Passion Translation captures this in Joel 2:25: 'I will restore to you the years that the swarming locust has eaten.'

Every seed contains the full potential of what it will become. Within an acorn lies a mighty oak. Within a tiny grape seed lies a sprawling vineyard. But there is a seed more powerful than any natural seed—the imperishable seed of divine life. This seed doesn't just carry potential; it carries the very nature of God Himself.

The Mirror Bible illuminates this profound reality in 1 Peter 1:23: "You are born again not from a seed that can perish, but from an imperishable seed, through the living and enduring word of God." This isn't metaphorical language—it's describing the actual transmission of divine life. Just as physical DNA carries the complete pattern for physical life, this imperishable seed carries the complete pattern of divine life.

The Passion Translation brings out this reality in 2 Peter 1:4: "As a result of this, he has given you magnificent promises that are beyond all price, so that through the power of these tremendous promises you can experience partnership with the divine nature." Notice the present tense—not will experience, but can experience. The seed of divine life isn't something waiting to germinate in the future; it's already active within us.

Think about how a seed works. It doesn't need anything added to it—it contains everything necessary for its full expression. It simply needs the right conditions to manifest what's already within it. The Mirror Bible captures this truth in Colossians 2:9-10: "All the fullness of deity dwells bodily in him and you are completely filled in him." We don't need to add anything to what we've received—we simply need to let what's already within us manifest.

The Nature of Imperishable Seed

Consider how different quantum particles are from classical objects. While classical objects degrade over time, quantum states remain unchanged until observed. Similarly, God's seed operates by different laws than natural seeds—it's eternally potent, immune to decay, operating by divine rather than natural principles.

What makes God's seed different from every other seed? The Mirror Bible expresses this uniqueness in 1 John 3:9: "Those born of God carry his DNA; his seed remains permanently within them." Unlike natural seeds that can decay or fail to germinate,

God's seed is imperishable—it cannot fail, cannot die, cannot be corrupted. Its nature is as eternal as God Himself.

The Passion Translation illuminates another aspect of this seed in John 1:12-13: "But those who embraced him and took hold of his name were given authority to become the children of God! He gave this authority to all who were born not of blood, nor of the desire or will of man, but of God." This seed doesn't operate by natural laws or human effort—it functions by divine life itself.

Consider how Jesus described this reality in John 3. The Passion Translation renders His words to Nicodemus: "I tell you the truth, unless you are born again from above by God's Spirit, you will never be able to enter into God's kingdom realm. For the natural realm can only give birth to things that are natural, but the Spirit gives birth to supernatural life!" The imperishable seed produces supernatural life because it carries supernatural DNA.

This seed operates with absolute certainty because it carries God's own nature. The Mirror Bible expresses this in Hebrews 10:23: "He who promised is faithful." The seed's effectiveness doesn't depend on our faithfulness but on His nature. Just as an apple seed can only produce an apple tree because that's its nature, God's seed can only produce divine life because that's His nature.

Think about how different this is from religious effort or moral improvement. We're not trying to become something through effort—we're carrying something that will inevitably express itself because that's its nature. The Mirror Bible captures this in Philippians 2:13: "God is working in you, giving you the desire and the power to do what pleases him." The seed produces both the desire and the ability.

Even more remarkable is the seed's relationship to time. While natural seeds operate within time—growing, developing, producing fruit in seasons—the imperishable seed carries eternal life itself. The Passion Translation renders 1 John 5:11-12: "This is the testimony: God has given us eternal life, and this life is in his Son. Whoever has the Son has life!" This isn't just endless duration—it's the very quality of God's own life.

Divine DNA in Action

Like how stem cells contain the potential to develop into any type of body tissue while maintaining their essential nature, divine DNA contains the potential for every expression of divine life while remaining unchangeably divine.

Just as physical DNA actively shapes every aspect of our physical being—from eye color to height to personality traits—divine DNA actively shapes our spiritual nature. The Mirror Bible expresses this dynamic reality in 2 Peter 1:3-4: "His divine power has already given us everything we need for life and godliness... He has given us his very great and precious promises, so that through them you may participate in the divine nature." Notice the present tense—this isn't future potential; it's present activity.

Think about how a child naturally manifests their parents' characteristics without effort or instruction. A child doesn't try to have their father's laugh or their mother's gestures—these expressions flow naturally from shared DNA. The Passion Translation captures this natural expression in 1 John 4:17: "As he is, so are we in this world." We're not trying to imitate God—we're expressing His nature that's within us.

The Mirror Bible illuminates how this works in Galatians 2:20: "I am crucified with Christ: nevertheless I live; yet not I, but Christ lives in me: and the life which I now live in the flesh I live by the faith of the Son of God." The divine life within us isn't passive—it's actively expressing itself through our humanity. Like a vine expressing its life through its branches, Christ expresses His life through us.

This divine DNA operates with sovereign independence from our efforts or understanding. The Passion Translation renders John 3:8: "The wind blows wherever it wants. Just as you can hear the wind but can't tell where it comes from or where it is going, so you can't explain how people are born of the Spirit." We don't control or direct this divine life—we participate in its natural expression.

Consider how this transforms our understanding of spiritual growth. We're not trying to become something we're not—we're allowing what's already within us to manifest. The Mirror Bible expresses this in 2 Corinthians 3:18: "We all, with unveiled face, beholding as in a mirror the glory of the Lord, are being transformed into the same image from glory to glory." The transformation happens naturally as we align with the divine life within us.

Even our desires are being shaped by this divine DNA. The Passion Translation captures this in Philippians 2:13: "God himself is at work in you, inspiring you to want those things which please him and to work for them." Just as physical DNA influences our natural preferences and inclinations, divine DNA shapes our spiritual desires and motivations.

Full Pattern of Divine Life

Just as a natural seed contains the complete blueprint for the entire plant—roots, stem, leaves, flowers, fruit—God's seed contains the complete pattern of divine life. The Mirror Bible expresses this completeness in Colossians 2:9-10: "All the fullness of deity dwells bodily in him and you are completely filled in him." Nothing needs to be added; the seed contains everything.

The Passion Translation illuminates this fullness in 2 Peter 1:3: "Everything we could ever need for life and godliness has already been deposited in us by his divine power." Notice the comprehensiveness—everything we could ever need. Not some things, not most things, but everything. The seed contains the complete pattern of divine life.

Think about how an acorn contains not just the pattern for one oak tree, but potentially an entire forest. Within that single seed lies the capability to reproduce its life endlessly. The Mirror Bible captures this reproductive power in John 12:24: "Unless a grain of wheat falls into the ground and dies, it remains alone. But if it dies, it produces many more seeds." The divine seed within us carries the same reproductive potential—it can multiply divine life endlessly.

This pattern includes every aspect of God's nature. The Passion Translation renders Ephesians 3:19: "Then you will be empowered to discover what every holy one experiences—the great magnitude of the astonishing love of Christ in all its dimensions. How deeply intimate and far-reaching is his love! How enduring and inclusive it is!" The seed contains not just part of God's love, but its full dimensionality.

Consider how comprehensive this pattern is. The Mirror Bible expresses it in 1 John 4:17: "The same love that he is, we are in this world!" We're not getting a diluted version or partial pattern—we're receiving the same love that He is. The seed contains the complete pattern of divine love, divine wisdom, divine power, divine nature.

Even more remarkably, this pattern includes our unique expression of divine life. The Mirror Bible illuminates this in Ephesians 2:10: "We are his poetry, we are the words of his story." Just as every oak tree from the same type of acorn is unique, each of us manifests divine life in our own unique way. The pattern includes both the universal nature of divine life and its personal expression through us.

Manifesting the Seed's Potential

How does the perfect pattern within God's seed manifest in our experience? The Mirror Bible illuminates this process in 2 Corinthians 3:18: "In him, every face mirrors the glory of the Lord. We are transfigured by the Spirit of the Lord in our constant beholding, from glory to glory; the image is restored in our thoughts according to the Original." The manifestation happens naturally as we behold—as we become aware of and align with the divine life within us.

Think about how a seed manifests its potential. It doesn't strive or struggle—it simply responds to the right conditions. The Passion Translation captures this natural unfolding in Mark 4:26-28: "God's kingdom realm is like someone spreading seed on the ground. He goes to bed and gets up day after day, and as the seeds sprout and grow tall, he doesn't know how it happens. All by itself, the earth produces a harvest—first the green stem, then the head on the stalk, and then the fully developed grain in the head."

This doesn't mean we're passive in the process. The Mirror Bible expresses our participation in Philippians 2:12-13: "Continue to work out your salvation with awe and reverence, for the happy certainty is that God is energizing you, causing you to desire and to work effectively motivated by his good pleasure!" We participate by aligning with and yielding to the divine life within us.

Consider how this differs from religious effort. We're not trying to become something we're not—we're allowing what's already within us to express itself. The Passion Translation renders Romans 8:11: "And if the Spirit of him who raised Jesus from the dead lives in you, he who raised Christ from the dead will also give life to your mortal bodies through his Spirit, who lives in you." The same power that raised Christ is actively giving life to our entire being.

Even our challenges and difficulties serve this manifestation process. The Mirror Bible illuminates this in 2 Corinthians 4:17:

"Our momentary light affliction is far outweighed by the most amazing eternal weight of glory that is about to be unveiled within us." Every circumstance becomes an opportunity for divine life to manifest through us.

This manifestation affects every aspect of our being—spirit, soul, and body. The Passion Translation expresses this comprehensive transformation in 1 Thessalonians 5:23: "Now, may the God of peace and harmony set you apart, making you completely holy. And may your entire being—spirit, soul, and body—be kept completely flawless in the appearing of our Lord Jesus, the Anointed One." The seed's potential manifests in our complete humanity.

Living from Divine Nature

What does it mean to live daily from the reality of God's seed within us? The Mirror Bible expresses this practical reality in 2 Peter 1:4: "He has given us all that we need to lead a godly lifestyle; these precious and magnificent promises have been fulfilled in our association with him. You are now participating in the divine nature!" This isn't about trying to live a divine life—it's about letting divine life live through us.

Think about how naturally a vine expresses its life through its branches. Jesus used this very image, and The Passion Translation captures it beautifully in John 15:4-5: "So you must remain in life-union with me, for I remain in life-union with you. For as a branch can't bear fruit by itself unless it remains attached to the vine, so neither can you bear fruit unless you remain in life-union with me. I am the sprouting vine and you're my branches. As you live in union with me as your source, fruitfulness will stream from within you."

Let's see how this works in everyday situations:

In Decision-Making: Just as a bird naturally knows how to build its nest without instruction, divine nature within you naturally knows how to navigate life's choices. Instead of anxiously weighing pros and cons, you can rest in the divine wisdom that's already expressing through you.

In Workplace Challenges: Like how your body naturally knows how to heal a cut without your conscious direction, divine life naturally knows how to handle situations as they arise. A teacher finds creative solutions flowing naturally in the classroom; a businessperson discovers innovative approaches in negotiathions; a parent finds patience arising spontaneously in challenging moments.

In Creative Endeavors: Consider how a master musician stops thinking about individual notes and simply lets the music flow. Similarly, when we live from divine nature, creativity flows naturally—whether we're cooking a meal, solving a problem, or helping a friend.

In Relationships: Just as a healthy tree naturally produces fruit without straining, divine love naturally expresses itself in our interactions. You might find yourself responding with unexpected wisdom to a friend's crisis, or expressing patience in situations that would normally trigger frustration.

In Spiritual Growth: Rather than following a set of rules or trying to measure your progress, you begin to notice divine characteristics naturally emerging—like how a flower naturally turns toward the sun without being told to do so.

This living from divine nature transforms how we approach every aspect of life. The Mirror Bible illuminates this in 2 Corinthians 5:17: "In Christ, every person discovers their true identity! The old is gone; look—what has become new is of the essence of God!" We're not trying to improve the old nature—we're living from an entirely new nature, the divine nature itself.

Consider how this affects our daily choices. When facing decisions, we're not trying to figure out what God would want— we're letting His nature within us express itself naturally. The

Passion Translation renders Philippians 2:13: "God himself is at work in you, inspiring you to want those things which please him and to work for them." His seed within us produces both the desire and the ability.

Even our relationships are transformed when we live from divine nature. The Mirror Bible expresses this in 1 John 4:7: "Beloved, let us love one another, for love is from God, and whoever loves has been born of God and knows God." We're not trying to be more loving—we're letting divine love flow naturally from the seed within us.

Practical Steps for Living from Divine Nature

Begin each day by acknowledging the reality of God's seed within you. Before facing any challenges or tasks, remind yourself that you carry divine nature. The Mirror Bible expresses this in Colossians 1:27: "Christ in you, the hope of glory!"

When facing challenges, instead of trying to generate strength or wisdom, rest in the divine nature within you. The Passion Translation affirms this in 2 Peter 1:3: "Everything we could ever need for life and complete devotion to God has already been deposited in us by his divine power."

In relationships, practice letting divine love flow naturally rather than trying to manufacture love. The Mirror Bible guides us: "The love of God is poured out in our hearts by the Holy Spirit given to us" (Romans 5:5).

Let your work flow from divine creativity rather than human effort. The Mirror Bible reminds us in Ephesians 2:10 that we are "his poetry... created in Christ Jesus."

Chapter Summary

God's imperishable seed within us contains the complete pattern of divine life. This isn't metaphorical—it's the actual transmission of divine nature. Like every seed, it naturally produces after its kind, manifesting the life of God through our humanity. We don't need to strive to become something we're not; we simply need to align with and live from the divine nature that's already within us. This seed cannot fail because it carries God's own nature, and it will inevitably express itself as we learn to live from its reality. Just as an apple seed contains not only the blueprint for a single apple tree but the potential for an entire orchard, this divine seed within us carries the full capacity for God's life to be expressed and multiplied through us. Understanding this truth shifts us from trying to attain divine nature to simply allowing what's already within us to grow and manifest naturally through our unique personality and expression.

Reflection Questions

1. How does understanding that you carry God's imperishable seed change how you view your spiritual growth?

2. What would change in your daily life if you consistently lived from divine nature rather than human effort?

3. How might your relationships transform if you let divine love flow naturally through God's seed within you?

4. What areas of your life most need to shift from striving to allowing divine nature to express itself?

5. How can you practically begin to live more consistently from the reality of God's seed within you?

Chapter 5

The Mystery of Theosis

Transformation into Divine Nature

In the heart of the Sahara Desert, there's a remarkable phenomenon known as "desert roses." These beautiful crystal formations look exactly like roses, yet they're made entirely of sand and minerals. Through a mysterious process, common sand is transformed into something that perfectly mirrors the pattern of a living flower. This natural wonder offers us a glimpse into an even greater mystery—how humanity is transformed into the very image of God Himself.

The early church father Athanasius expressed this profound mystery in a statement that would shake the foundations of how we understand our relationship with God: "God became man so that man might become divine." This wasn't casual theological speculation—it was a declaration of the purpose behind the incarnation itself. The Mirror Bible captures this revolutionary truth in 2 Peter 1:4: "He has given us all that we need to lead a godly lifestyle; these precious and magnificent promises have been fulfilled in our association with him. You are now participating in the divine nature!"

Consider the implications: Just as Jesus is fully divine and fully human, we too are called to be fully human and participate in divine nature. This isn't about becoming "little gods" or losing our humanity—it's about fulfilling humanity's original design. The Passion Translation illuminates this in Genesis 1:26-27: "Then God said, 'Let us make humans in our image, to be like us... So God created humans in his own image; in the image of God he created them; male and female he created them.'"

This mystery of theosis—our participation in divine nature—was understood deeply by the early church. They saw it not as an optional "advanced teaching" but as the very heart of salvation itself. Gregory of Nazianzus, another early church father, declared, "Let us become as Christ is, since Christ became as we are; let us become divine for His sake, since He became human for our sake."

Let me share a story that illustrates this truth. A master sculptor once took on an apprentice who was struggling with a particularly challenging piece of marble. The apprentice kept trying to force his vision onto the stone, becoming increasingly frustrated. The master stepped in and said, "Your mistake is thinking you need to make this marble into something it's not. Look deeper—the masterpiece is already there, waiting to be revealed. Your job isn't to create something new but to unveil what's already present."

The Divine-Human Reality

In the mountains of California grows an extraordinary tree—the Giant Sequoia. These magnificent beings can live over 3,000 years and reach heights of 300 feet. Yet something even more remarkable happens beneath their bark. Over centuries, these trees actually fuse their root systems together, creating an interconnected network that shares nutrients, water, and even information. While remaining distinct trees, they become one living system. This natural wonder offers us a picture of the divine-human reality—distinct yet completely united.

In mathematics and nature, there exists a fascinating phenomenon called fractals—patterns that repeat themselves at every scale, from microscopic to cosmic. A small piece contains the same pattern as the whole, whether you zoom in or out. Ferns demonstrate this perfectly—each tiny leaflet mirrors the pattern of the entire frond. This natural wonder illustrates the mystery of theosis—how we carry and express divine nature. The Mirror

Bible expresses this reality in 1 John 4:17: 'As He is, so are we in this world!'

From the spiraling pattern of galaxies to the branching of trees, from the structure of snowflakes to the rhythm of heartbeats, fractals reveal how the same divine pattern can manifest at every scale while maintaining its essential nature. Just as each branch of a tree contains the pattern of the whole tree, each expression of divine nature through us maintains the fullness of divine life.

Just as a fractal pattern maintains its essential nature regardless of scale, we manifest divine nature without diminishing or altering its essence. Each of us uniquely expresses the same divine pattern while maintaining the complete nature. The Passion Translation captures this in 2 Peter 1:4: 'As a result of this, he has given you magnificent promises that are beyond all price, so that through them you can experience partnership with the divine nature.'"

The Mirror Bible expresses this profound union In 1 Corinthians 6:17: "The one being joined to the Lord exists as one spirit with him!" Just as Jesus is fully divine and fully human without confusion or division, we too are called to this divine-human reality. We don't lose our humanity—we find its true fulfilment in union with divine nature.

Consider the mystery of light. In quantum physics, light exhibits what scientists call "wave-particle duality"—it's both a wave and a particle simultaneously, without contradiction. This scientific reality helps us understand how we can be both fully human and participants in divine nature without contradiction. The Passion Translation captures this dual reality in 1 John 4:17: "As he is, so are we in this world!"

Let me share a story that illuminates this truth. In a remote monastery, a young monk once approached his elder with a troubled heart. "Father," he said, "I keep trying to balance my human nature and divine nature, but it feels like I'm constantly switching between the two." The elder smiled and led him to the monastery garden where roses were blooming. "Look at this rose," he said. "Is it less a rose because it carries the life of the sun within it? Or is it more truly a rose because it manifests the light it receives? Your humanity isn't diminished by divine life—it's fulfilled by it."

This divine-human reality isn't just theoretical—it's the very essence of our inheritance in Christ. The Mirror Bible illuminates this in Colossians 2:9-10: "All the fullness of deity dwells bodily in him and you are completely filled in him." Notice the parallel—just as deity dwells bodily in Christ, we are completely filled in Him. We're not becoming something alien to our nature; we're becoming what we were always meant to be.

Think about how a prism interacts with light. The prism doesn't become the light, yet it's filled with light and refracts it in unique and beautiful ways. Each prism, depending on its cut and clarity, expresses the same light differently. The Passion Translation expresses this reality in 2 Corinthians 3:18: "We can all draw close to him with the veil removed from our faces. And with no veil we all become like mirrors who brightly reflect the glory of the Lord Jesus."

Even our daily experiences reflect this divine-human reality. When you're deeply in love, you remain distinctly yourself while being profoundly influenced and transformed by the one you love. When you're caught up in creating art or music, you're simultaneously more yourself and more than yourself. These human experiences hint at the greater reality of our divine-human nature.

The early church father Irenaeus expressed this beautifully: "The glory of God is a human being fully alive." He understood that our humanity reaches its fullest expression not by suppressing it in favor of divinity, but by allowing it to be permeated with divine life. The Mirror Bible captures this in 2 Corinthians 4:7: "We have this treasure in earthen vessels, that the excellency of the power may be of God, and not of us."

Beyond Religious Effort

On Japan's Yakushima Island grows a remarkable cedar tree known as the Jōmon Sugi, estimated to be between 2,000 and 6,000 years old. What's fascinating is that this ancient tree has never tried to be a cedar—it simply manifests what it is. It has faced typhoons, survived centuries of climate changes, and grown to magnificent proportions not through effort, but through naturally expressing its inherent nature. This offers us a profound picture of how divine life manifests—not through religious striving, but through natural expression of what we already are.

Consider how differently a professional athlete performs compared to an amateur. The amateur thinks about every movement, while the professional flows naturally, having internalized the game so deeply it becomes second nature. This illustrates the difference between religious effort and natural expression of divine life.

Consider the difference between a person learning to act like a parent and a person who is a parent. The actor must constantly think about what a parent would do, trying to replicate parental behavior. But an actual parent naturally expresses parental love because that's who they are. The Mirror Bible captures this difference in Galatians 4:6-7: "The proof of your sonship is the fact that God sent forth the Spirit of his Son into our hearts, crying, 'Abba, Father!' Therefore, you are no longer a slave but a son, and if a son, then an heir of God through Christ."

Let me share a story that illuminates this truth. A young ballet dancer was struggling with a particularly challenging role. She practiced relentlessly, counting every step, analyzing every movement, yet something was missing. Her instructor noticed her frustration and said, "Stop trying to dance the steps and let the music dance you." When she finally let go of her careful control and allowed the music to flow through her, she discovered a grace and beauty that no amount of effort could produce.

This is the difference between religion and theosis. Religion says, "Try harder to be like God." Theosis says, "Let the divine life within you express itself naturally." The Passion Translation expresses this in Philippians 2:13: "God himself is at work in you, inspiring you to want those things which please him and to work for them." Notice the order—God's work produces both the desire and the ability.

Think about how a newborn baby breathes. The baby doesn't attend breathing classes or study respiratory techniques—they simply breathe because that's what they're designed to do. In the same way, divine life expresses itself naturally through us when we stop trying to manufacture it. The Mirror Bible illuminates this in 2 Corinthians 3:18: "We are transfigured by the Spirit of the Lord in our constant beholding, from glory to glory."

Even in nature, we see this principle at work. Consider how a flower opens to the sun. It doesn't strain or struggle—it naturally responds to the light. The early church father Maximus the Confessor understood this when he wrote, "A human being is one who has united love to natural power, having persuaded inclination to follow nature." He knew that our transformation comes not through forcing ourselves to be something we're not, but through aligning with what we truly are in Christ.

The Passion Translation captures this natural expression in 1 John 4:19: "Our love for others is our grateful response to the love God first demonstrated toward us." Notice again the order—we don't generate love through effort; we naturally express the love we've received.

This understanding transforms how we approach spiritual growth. Instead of asking, "What would Jesus do?" as if He's an external example to imitate, we begin asking, "What is Christ, who lives in me, doing?" The Mirror Bible expresses this internal reality in Colossians 3:4: "Christ is your life!" Not Christ showing us how to live, but Christ actually being our life.

Think of how water reflects the sky. The water doesn't strain to create the reflection—it simply remains still and naturally mirrors what's above it. This is why the Desert Fathers emphasized stillness (*hesychia*) as the key to transformation. Not a passive stillness, but an alert receptivity that allows divine life to manifest naturally.

Union and Distinction

In the heart of every rainbow lies a profound paradox. When sunlight passes through water droplets, it remains pure light while simultaneously manifesting as distinct colors. The colors aren't separate from the light—they are the light expressed in unique ways. Yet each color maintains its distinct identity while remaining inseparable from the source. This natural phenomenon offers us a beautiful picture of our union with God—complete oneness while maintaining distinct identity.

The Mirror Bible expresses this mysterious union in John 17:21-23: "That they all may be one, as You, Father, are in Me, and I in You; that they also may be one in Us... I in them, and You in Me; that they may be made perfect in one." This isn't mere cooperation or alignment—it's actual union, yet without the loss of distinct identity.

Let me share a story that illuminates this truth. A master musician once explained to his students the mystery of improvisation in jazz. "When you're truly in the flow," he said, "you're not thinking about what notes to play next. You're so one with the music that it plays through you. Yet paradoxically, that's when your unique voice emerges most clearly. The more you surrender to the music, the more distinctly you express yourself." This perfectly illustrates how union with divine life enhances rather than diminishes our unique identity.

Consider how marriage works at its best. The Passion Translation renders Ephesians 5:31-32: "'For this reason a man will leave his father and mother and be united to his wife, and the two will become one flesh.' This is a profound mystery—but I am talking about Christ and the church." In a healthy marriage, two people become one while remaining distinctly themselves. In fact, true marital union often brings out the unique qualities of each person more fully.

The early church father Gregory of Nyssa used the metaphor of iron in fire to explain this union. When iron is placed in fire, it becomes completely permeated with the fire's properties—heat, light, and energy. The iron remains iron, yet it's so united with the fire that you can't separate the two. The Mirror Bible captures this reality in 1 Corinthians 6:17: "The one being joined to the Lord exists as one spirit with him!"

Think about how ocean waves work. Each wave is distinctly itself, with its own shape, size, and movement. Yet no wave is separate from the ocean—it's the ocean expressing itself in that unique form. The Passion Translation illuminates this in Acts 17:28: "For in him we live and move and have our being." We're not separate entities trying to connect with God—we're distinct expressions of divine life.

This understanding transforms how we view our individuality. Many fear that union with God will erase their personality, like a drop of water losing itself in the ocean. But the reality is quite the opposite. The Mirror Bible expresses this in 1 Corinthians 15:10: "By the grace of God I am what I am!" Union with divine life doesn't diminish our uniqueness—it establishes and enhances it.

Consider how a prism works with light. When pure white light passes through a prism, it doesn't lose any of its essential nature, yet it manifests in unique and beautiful ways depending on the prism's specific characteristics. Each prism produces its own distinct pattern while remaining completely one with the light. The early church father Maximus the Confessor described this as "unity without confusion, distinction without separation."

Even in nature, we see this principle at work in the way grafted branches function. A grafted branch maintains its distinct fruit-bearing characteristics while being completely united with the life of the tree. The Passion Translation captures this organic union in John 15:4: "So you must remain in life-union with me, for I remain in life-union with you. For as a branch can't bear fruit by itself unless it remains attached to the vine, so neither can you bear fruit unless you remain in life-union with me."

Manifesting Divine Nature

Deep within California's Mojave Desert lies a remarkable phenomenon—the sailing stones of Death Valley. These rocks, some weighing hundreds of pounds, move across the desert floor leaving long tracks behind them, yet no one sees them move. Scientists finally discovered that under the right conditions, a delicate combination of water, ice, and wind creates an environment where these stones glide effortlessly across the ground. What seemed impossible happens naturally when the right conditions are present. This offers us a picture of how divine nature manifests through us—not through force or effort, but through the presence of the right conditions.

The Mirror Bible expresses this natural manifestation in 2 Peter 1:3-4: "His divine power has already given us everything we need for life and godliness... enabling you to experience partnership with the divine nature." Notice the order—we're not trying to achieve divine nature; we're learning to experience what's already present.

Let me share a story that illuminates this truth. A master glassblower once took on an apprentice who was struggling to create beautiful pieces. The apprentice was strong and technically skilled, but his pieces lacked life. The master observed him for a while, then said, "Your problem is that you're trying to force the glass into shape. Glass doesn't respond to force—it responds to heat. When it's hot enough, it flows naturally into beautiful forms. Your job is to maintain the right temperature and work with the glass's natural properties." This apprentice's journey mirrors our own—we're learning to maintain the conditions where divine nature naturally flows through us.

Consider how a Chinese bamboo tree grows. For the first four years after planting, nothing appears to happen—all the growth is happening underground in an extensive root system. Then, in the fifth year, the bamboo can grow up to 90 feet in just six weeks. The Passion Translation captures this pattern in Colossians 3:3-4: "Your secret life is now hidden in God as you are placed into the revelation of the life of Christ. And when Christ who is your life is revealed, then you will also be revealed with him in glory!"

The early church father Symeon the New Theologian described this manifestation like sunrise: "Just as the sun rises gradually— first a glimmer of light, then the full disk appears—so does Christ, the Sun of righteousness, rise in us." The Mirror Bible illuminates this gradual dawning in 2 Corinthians 3:18: "We are transfigured by the Spirit of the Lord in our constant beholding, from glory to glory."

Think about how a hologram works. Unlike a photograph, every piece of a hologram contains the whole image—some pieces might be clearer than others, but the complete pattern is present in each part. Similarly, divine nature isn't parceled out to us in pieces—the whole is present, manifesting with increasing clarity as we grow in awareness. The Passion Translation expresses this in Ephesians 3:19: "Then you will be empowered to discover what every holy one experiences—the great magnitude of the astonishing love of Christ in all its dimensions."

This manifestation affects every aspect of our being. Like water taking on the temperature of fire beneath it, our thoughts, emotions, desires, and actions naturally begin to express divine nature as we remain in union. The Mirror Bible captures this comprehensive transformation in 1 Thessalonians 5:23: "May the God of peace himself sanctify you completely, and may your whole spirit and soul and body be kept blameless at the coming of our Lord Jesus Christ."

Even our daily experiences begin to shift. Instead of trying to be loving, we find love flowing naturally. Instead of striving for peace, we discover we are peace. The early church father Gregory Palamas described this as becoming "uncreated by grace"—not losing our created nature but having it so permeated with divine life that it naturally expresses divine qualities.

Living in Theosis

In the highlands of Scotland grows a remarkable tree known as the Fortingall Yew. What appears to be a cluster of separate trees is actually one living organism that has grown for over 3,000 years. Over centuries, its massive trunk hollowed out and divided into what looks like distinct trees, yet they remain one living being sharing the same root system. This ancient wonder offers us a picture of living in theosis—appearing distinct while sharing one divine life.

The Mirror Bible expresses this reality of living from divine nature in Colossians 3:3-4: "Your life is now hidden with Christ in God. Christ is your life!" This isn't a distant goal to achieve but a present reality to manifest. Like the Fortingall Yew, we're not trying to connect to divine life—we're learning to live from the one life we already share.

Let me share a story that illuminates this truth. A young apprentice asked his spiritual father, "How do I live this divine life?" The elder took him to a stream and asked him to collect water in his hands. As the apprentice cupped his hands, the elder said, "Notice three things. First, your hands must be empty to receive the water. Second, the water takes the shape of your hands while remaining water. Third, the water flows continuously—you can't store it, only live in its constant flow." This simple lesson captures the essence of living in theosis.

Think about how a surfer rides a wave. The surfer doesn't create the wave's power or try to control its direction. Instead, they learn to align with the wave's natural movement, becoming one with its flow while maintaining their distinct balance and expression. The Passion Translation captures this dynamic in Acts 17:28: "For in him we live and move and have our being." We're not generating divine life—we're learning to move with it.

The early church father Maximus the Confessor described this as "natural movement according to nature." Just as everything in nature moves according to its inherent properties, we learn to move according to the divine nature within us. The Mirror Bible illuminates this in Philippians 2:13: "God is working in you, giving you the desire and the power to do what pleases him."

Let's see how theosis naturally manifests in everyday situations:

In Family Life: Like how a mother naturally knows her child's cry among hundreds of others, divine awareness flows naturally through your relationships. You might find yourself understanding family members' needs before they express them, or responding with wisdom that surprises even you.

In Work Situations: Just as a master chef instinctively knows when to adjust heat or add ingredients without measuring, divine life expresses naturally through your work. A teacher spontaneously finds the right words to reach a struggling student; a business leader intuitively navigates complex decisions; a craftsperson's hands move with inspired precision.

In Creative Activities: Consider how an experienced pianist's fingers find the right keys without conscious thought. Similarly, divine creativity flows naturally—whether you're solving a problem, designing a project, or finding innovative solutions. You're not trying to be creative; you're expressing the Creator's life within you.

In Crisis Moments: Like how a trained lifeguard responds instinctively to an emergency, divine wisdom manifests naturally in challenging situations. You find yourself responding with unexpected grace under pressure, or speaking words of life that could only come from divine nature expressing through you.

In Daily Routines: Even mundane activities become expressions of divine life. Making breakfast becomes an act of love; daily commutes become opportunities for presence; routine tasks become moments of communion. Like a dancer who moves gracefully even when alone, divine life expresses naturally in every moment.

Practical Steps for Living in Theosis

Begin each day with recognition. Before facing any tasks or challenges, acknowledge the reality that Christ is your life. The Mirror Bible expresses this in Galatians 2:20: "I no longer live, but Christ lives in me." This isn't positive thinking—it's aligning with reality.

Practice presence in ordinary moments. Like a tree continuously drawing nourishment from its roots, maintain awareness of your union with divine life. The Passion Translation renders John 15:4: "So you must remain in life-union with me, for I remain in life-union with you."

Let relationships become opportunities for divine expression. Instead of trying to manufacture love or patience, allow divine nature to flow naturally through your unique personality. The Mirror Bible guides us: "The love of God is poured out in our hearts by the Holy Spirit given to us" (Romans 5:5).

Face challenges from union rather than separation. Like a branch drawing life from the vine, face every situation from your connection to divine life. The Mirror Bible reminds us in 2 Corinthians 4:7: "We have this treasure in earthen vessels, that the excellency of the power may be of God, and not of us."

Let your work flow from divine energy. Instead of striving in your own strength, allow divine life to express itself through your activities. The Passion Translation expresses this in Colossians

1:29: "I labor with all the energy that he powerfully works within me."

Even in rest, maintain awareness of union. Like a wave that's never separate from the ocean, know that you're never disconnected from divine life. The early church father Gregory of Nyssa described this as "eternal progress in God"—constant participation in divine life that becomes increasingly natural.

Consider how a master musician becomes one with their instrument. After years of practice, there's no separation between musician and music—they're so united that music flows effortlessly. This is living in theosis—so united with divine life that it naturally expresses itself through everything we do.

The Mirror Bible captures this seamless living in 1 John 4:17: "The same love that he is, we are in this world!" Notice the present tense—not becoming, not striving, but being. This is theosis— natural expression of the divine life we share.

Chapter Summary

Theosis isn't about becoming something we're not—it's about manifesting what we already are in Christ. Through the incarnation, God became human so that humans might participate in divine nature. This isn't mere imitation or effort; it's natural expression of the divine life we share. Like a branch naturally expressing the life of the vine, we learn to let divine nature flow through our unique personality and circumstances. The mystery of theosis is that we become most truly human as we participate most fully in divine life. Just as iron placed in fire begins to take on the properties of fire while remaining iron, we participate in divine nature while remaining uniquely ourselves. This transforms our understanding of spiritual growth—instead of striving to achieve divinity, we're awakening to and expressing the divine-human nature already established in Christ. Through this participation, we discover that our humanity isn't something to transcend but something to fulfill through union with divine life.

Reflection Questions

1. How does understanding theosis change your approach to spiritual growth?

2. What areas of your life most need to shift from effort to natural expression of divine life?

3. How might your relationships transform if you lived consistently from divine nature?

4. What practical steps can you take to maintain awareness of your union with divine life?

5. How does seeing yourself as a participant in divine nature change your daily experience?

Chapter 6

The Journey from Slavery to Sonship

Our Journey to Inheritance

Every great story of transformation follows a journey. Consider how a monarch butterfly emerges from its chrysalis—it must pass through distinct stages, each essential to its ultimate expression of freedom and beauty. But perhaps no journey better illustrates our transformation from slavery to sonship than Israel's exodus from Egypt to the Promised Land. This wasn't just a historical event; it was a prophetic pattern of every believer's journey from bondage to inheritance.

The Mirror Bible illuminates this pattern in Galatians 4:1-7: "As long as the heir is a child, he does not differ from a slave, though he is owner of everything... But when the fullness of the time came, God sent forth His Son... so that He might redeem those who were under the Law, that we might receive the adoption as sons." Like Israel, we journey from slavery to sonship, from mere servants to mature heirs.

Consider the stages of Israel's journey: slavery in Egypt, the Passover lamb, crossing the Red Sea, wilderness training, crossing Jordan, and finally entering the Promised Land. The Passion Translation captures this progression in Exodus 6:6-8: "I will bring you out from under the burdens of the Egyptians, and I will deliver you from slavery to them, and I will redeem you with an outstretched arm... and I will take you to be my people, and I will be your God... And I will bring you into the land that I swore to give to Abraham, to Isaac, and to Jacob."

This journey reflects our own path from separation consciousness to son consciousness. Like a seed breaking through layers of soil to reach sunlight, we break through layers of false identity to emerge in the full light of our true nature. But this emergence isn't instant—it follows a divine pattern that respects our need for growth and development.

From Egypt to Freedom

Every Exodus begins with a revelation. For Israel, it started when Moses encountered God at the burning bush. For us, it begins with a revelation of our true identity. The Mirror Bible expresses this awakening in Exodus 3:7: "I have surely seen the affliction of my people... and have heard their cry because of their taskmasters, for I know their sorrows." Notice God's language—"my people." Even in their slavery, He saw them as His own.

Consider how different this is from the slave identity Israel had internalized. After generations in Egypt, they had come to see themselves as Pharaoh saw them—as slaves, as property, as less than. Many of us have similarly internalized false identities based on performance, approval, or circumstances. Like an elephant tethered by a rope it could easily break—but doesn't because it learned its "limitations" as a baby—we often remain bound by beliefs that no longer reflect reality.

Let me share a story that illuminates this truth. In a remote village, a young artist was known for creating beautiful sculptures from broken pieces of pottery. When asked about her unusual medium, she explained, "My grandfather taught me that nothing is truly broken—it's just waiting to be seen in a new way. These pieces aren't garbage; they're raw material for something beautiful." This perfectly illustrates how God sees us even in our "Egypt"—not as broken slaves, but as raw material for displaying His glory.

The Passion Translation captures this perspective in Exodus 6:5-6: "I have heard the groaning of the Israelites whom the Egyptians are enslaving, and I have remembered my covenant... Say therefore to the Israelites, 'I am the LORD, and I will bring you out from under the burdens of the Egyptians.'" God's liberation always begins with His remembrance of covenant, not our performance or worthiness.

Think about how a key works. The key doesn't create the lock's internal mechanism—it matches it, activating what's already there. Similarly, revelation doesn't create our identity as sons—it awakens us to what's already true. The Mirror Bible illuminates this in Galatians 4:9: "But now that you know God—or rather are known by God—how is it that you are turning back to those weak and miserable forces? Do you wish to be enslaved by them all over again?"

The journey from Egypt requires a Passover lamb. For Israel, it was a physical lamb whose blood marked their doorposts. For us, it's Christ, our Passover Lamb, whose finished work marks us permanently as God's own. The Passion Translation expresses this in 1 Corinthians 5:7: "For Christ, our Passover Lamb, has been sacrificed for us."

Consider the profound shift this represents. In Egypt, Israel worked to survive. After Passover, they lived from provision. In Egypt, they were defined by their slavery. After Passover, they were defined by their covenant. In Egypt, they served Pharaoh. After Passover, they served God as His firstborn son. The Mirror Bible captures this transformation in Romans 8:15: "The Spirit you received does not make you slaves, so that you live in fear again; rather, the Spirit you received brought about your adoption to sonship."

This exodus continues with a Red Sea crossing—a point of no return. For Israel, it meant the death of their slave identity as they watched Egypt's army drown. For us, it means seeing our old identity crucified with Christ. The early church fathers saw baptism as our Red Sea—a defining moment where we pass from death to life.

Yet, like Israel, many try to maintain a slave mentality even after liberation. The Mirror Bible expresses this tension in Galatians 5:1: "Christ has set us free to live a free life. So take your stand! Never again let anyone put a harness of slavery on you." Freedom isn't just a change of circumstance—it's a change of consciousness.

Think about how a spacecraft uses a gravity slingshot to break free from Earth's pull. It must reach a precise point where Earth's gravity actually propels it forward rather than holding it back. Similarly, there's a point in our journey where what once bound us becomes the very thing God uses to propel us into freedom. Every limitation, every bondage, every "Egypt" in our lives becomes material for displaying His glory.

Wilderness Training

In the heart of Death Valley lies a remarkable phenomenon known as the "sailing stones"—rocks that move across the desert floor leaving long tracks behind them, yet no one sees them move. Scientists discovered that under specific conditions involving thin sheets of ice and gentle winds, these heavy stones glide effortlessly across the desert. Similarly, the wilderness creates unique conditions where what seems impossible—the transformation of slave thinking into son thinking—happens naturally.

The Mirror Bible illuminates this transformative process in Deuteronomy 8:2: "Remember how the Lord your God led you all the way in the wilderness these forty years, to humble you and to test you in order to know what was in your heart." The wilderness isn't punishment—it's preparation. Like a greenhouse creating perfect conditions for growth, the wilderness creates an environment where our true identity can emerge.

Consider how different the wilderness was from Egypt. In Egypt, they could see their resources (even if they didn't own them). In the wilderness, they had to trust in invisible provision. In Egypt, they followed a predictable schedule. In the wilderness, they had to follow God's presence. In Egypt, they knew what to expect. In the wilderness, they had to live by faith rather than sight. The Passion Translation captures this shift in 2 Corinthians 5:7: "For we live by faith, not by sight."

Let me share a story that illuminates this truth. A master jeweler was training his apprentice in the art of working with gold. The apprentice was frustrated because the gold seemed to resist every attempt to shape it. The master explained, "Gold must first pass through fire. What seems like destruction is actually preparation. The heat doesn't destroy the gold—it reveals its true nature by removing what isn't gold." This perfectly illustrates how wilderness experiences remove what isn't consistent with our true identity.

Think about how an eagle trains its young to fly. It doesn't begin with flight school—it begins by disturbing the nest, making it uncomfortable. The Mirror Bible expresses this divine strategy in Deuteronomy 32:11: "Like an eagle that stirs up its nest and hovers over its young, that spreads its wings to catch them and carries them aloft." God's wilderness training often involves disturbing our comfortable slave mindsets.

The wilderness also reveals what we're truly trusting in. For Israel, every challenge exposed whether they were trusting God's word or their own resources. The Passion Translation renders Proverbs 3:5-6: "Trust in the LORD completely, and do not rely on your own opinions. With all your heart rely on him to guide you, and he will lead you in every decision you make." The wilderness strips away our illusion of self-sufficiency.

Consider how a caterpillar transforms in its chrysalis. What looks like destruction is actually reconstruction. The Mirror Bible captures this transformation process in 2 Corinthians 3:18: "We are transfigured by the Spirit of the Lord in our constant beholding, from glory to glory." The wilderness is our chrysalis— a protected space where slave thinking dissolves and son consciousness emerges.

Even Jesus experienced wilderness training. The Passion Translation expresses this in Luke 4:1-2: "Then Jesus, full of the Holy Spirit, returned from the Jordan River. He was led by the Spirit into the wilderness, where he was tempted by the devil for forty days." The wilderness wasn't about making Jesus something He wasn't—it was about establishing who He already was as Son.

The early church fathers saw the wilderness as essential training in trusting God's nature rather than our own efforts. When the Israelites faced thirst, God revealed Himself as living water. When they faced hunger, He revealed Himself as bread from heaven. Each challenge was an opportunity to know God's nature more deeply. The Mirror Bible illuminates this in Philippians 3:10: "I want to know Christ—yes, to know the power of his resurrection."

Crossing Jordan

Every journey has a point of no return—a threshold that, once crossed, changes everything. For Israel, this was the Jordan River. Unlike the Red Sea crossing that took them out of Egypt, the Jordan crossing took them into inheritance. The Mirror Bible captures this pivotal moment in Joshua 3:13: "And as soon as the priests who carry the ark of the LORD step into the Jordan, its waters flowing downstream will be cut off and stand up in a heap." This wasn't just a geographical transition—it was a consciousness transition.

Consider the profound difference between these two crossings. At the Red Sea, they fled from something (slavery). At Jordan, they stepped into something (inheritance). At the Red Sea, God parted the waters before they stepped in. At Jordan, the waters parted only after they stepped in. The Passion Translation illuminates this shift in Joshua 1:3: "I promise you what I promised Moses: 'Wherever you set foot, you will be on land I have given you.'"

Let me share a story that illustrates this truth. A master tightrope walker was training a new apprentice. The apprentice had mastered all the technical skills but still hesitated at crucial moments. The master explained, "The difference between a novice and a master isn't in knowing how to walk the rope—it's in knowing that you are a walker. When you cross that line in your mind, your body follows naturally." This perfectly captures the Jordan crossing—it's where we stop thinking like wanderers and start thinking like heirs.

Think about how a space shuttle breaks free from Earth's atmosphere. There's a precise point called "escape velocity" where the shuttle breaks free from gravitational pull. Before that point, it's fighting gravity. After that point, it's flying in its intended environment. The Mirror Bible expresses this transformation in Colossians 3:1-2: "Since, then, you have been raised with Christ, set your hearts on things above, where Christ is, seated at the right hand of God. Set your minds on things above, not on earthly things."

The Jordan crossing also required carrying the Ark of the Covenant—the symbol of God's presence and promise. The early church fathers saw this as a picture of carrying the consciousness of Christ's finished work. The Passion Translation renders 2 Corinthians 2:14: "God always makes his grace visible in Christ, who includes us as partners of his endless triumph." We cross our Jordan carrying the consciousness of victory already secured in Christ.

Consider how different this is from wilderness thinking. In the wilderness, they constantly looked back to Egypt, comparing their current challenges with their former slavery. After Jordan, they looked forward to inheritance, seeing challenges as opportunities to possess what was already theirs. The Mirror Bible captures this shift in Romans 8:37: "In all these things we are more than conquerors through him who loved us."

There's a profound detail in this Jordan crossing that's easily missed. The Mirror Bible captures this significant moment in Joshua 3:16: 'The waters which came down from upstream stood still, and rose in a heap very far away at Adam, the city that is beside Zaretan. So the waters that went down into the Sea of the Arabah, the Salt Sea, failed, and were cut off.'

Notice the symbolism: the waters were cut off all the way back to a town called Adam, while the waters flowing to the Dead Sea were completely stopped. This isn't mere geographical detail—it's a prophetic picture. The waters rolling back to Adam symbolizes how crossing Jordan cuts off the flow of Adam's fallen nature. The waters to the Dead Sea being stopped shows how death's power is cut off. In Christ, we cross over from Adam's nature (which leads to death) into new creation life. The Passion Translation illuminates this reality in 1 Corinthians 15:22: 'For as in Adam all die, so in Christ all will be made alive.'"

This crossing affects every area of life. Like a quantum particle that can't return to its previous state once it makes a quantum leap, crossing Jordan represents a consciousness shift that can't be reversed. The Passion Translation expresses this in Philippians 3:13-14: "But I focus on this one thing: Forgetting the past and looking forward to what lies ahead, I press on to reach the end of the race and receive the heavenly prize for which God, through Christ Jesus, is calling us."

Even the timing of the crossing was significant—during flood season when the Jordan was at its fullest. God often brings us to our Jordan when challenges seem greatest, because that's when the shift in consciousness is most dramatic. The Mirror Bible illuminates this in 2 Corinthians 12:9: "My grace is enough for you, for my power finds its full expression through your weakness."

Giants in the Land

When Israel first spied out the Promised Land, they saw giants and called themselves grasshoppers in comparison. Forty years later, facing the same giants, they saw themselves as sons and called the giants bread for their eating. The Mirror Bible captures this transformation in Numbers 14:9: "Only do not rebel against the

LORD. And do not fear the people of the land, for they are bread for us. Their protection has been removed from them, and the LORD is with us!" What changed wasn't the size of the giants—what changed was their consciousness of who they were.

Today's giants may not be physical Nephilim, but they're just as real: the giant of separation consciousness that makes us feel distant from God, the giant of performance-based acceptance that keeps us striving, the giant of orphan thinking that obscures our true identity. The Passion Translation illuminates our victory over these giants in 1 John 4:4: "Little children, you can be certain that you belong to God and have conquered them, for the One who is living in you is far greater than the one who is in the world."

Today's giants may not be physical Nephilim, but they're just as intimidating—often more so because they operate in our minds and hearts. The Mirror Bible expresses this reality in 2 Corinthians 10:4-5: 'The weapons we fight with are not weapons of the world... we demolish arguments and every pretension that sets itself up against the knowledge of God.' These giants often wear religious disguises: the giant of separation consciousness that makes us feel distant from God, the giant of performance-based acceptance that keeps us striving, the giant of condemnation that reminds us of past failures. Like the Israelites, we must see these giants not as obstacles but as bread for our eating—opportunities to demonstrate our true identity in Christ.

Let me share a story that illuminates this truth. A master martial artist was teaching his student about facing larger opponents. The student was focused on techniques to overcome size disadvantage. The master stopped him and said, "Your problem isn't your opponent's size—it's your consciousness of size. When you know who you are, your opponent's size becomes irrelevant. In fact, their size becomes leverage you can use." This perfectly illustrates how son-consciousness transforms our view of challenges.

Consider how David faced Goliath. The Mirror Bible expresses his inheritance consciousness in 1 Samuel 17:26: "Who is this uncircumcised Philistine that he should defy the armies of the living God?" Notice David didn't deny Goliath's size—he simply saw it from the perspective of his covenant identity. The giant's very size made him a bigger target for God's glory.

Think about how an aikido master uses an attacker's force to their advantage. The larger and more forceful the attack, the more energy is available for redirection. The Passion Translation captures this principle in Romans 8:28: "So we are convinced that every detail of our lives is continually woven together to fit into God's perfect plan of bringing good into our lives, for we are his lovers who have been called to fulfil his designed purpose."

The early church fathers saw these giants as opportunities rather than obstacles. Athanasius wrote, "The greater the trial, the greater the revelation of Christ's life through us." The Mirror Bible illuminates this perspective in 2 Corinthians 4:17: "Our momentary light affliction is far outweighed by the most amazing eternal weight of glory that is about to be unveiled within us."

Consider how different this is from slave thinking. Slaves see giants as proof of their weakness. Sons see giants as opportunities to demonstrate their inheritance. The Mirror Bible expresses this in Romans 8:37: "In all these things we are super conquerors through him who loved us!" Not just conquerors—super conquerors, because every challenge becomes an opportunity to manifest sonship.
Even our "giants" of the past—failures, wounds, limitations— become bread for our eating when seen through son-consciousness. Like a master composer who uses dissonance to create more beautiful harmony, God uses our challenges to display His glory through us. The Passion Translation renders Genesis 50:20: "Even though you intended to harm me, God intended it for good, and through my life has fulfilled his purpose of saving many lives."

Living as Mature Sons

In the world of classical music, there's a profound difference between a student musician and a master. The student is still conscious of every note, every technique, every rule. The master has internalized the music so completely that it flows naturally—they don't play the music; they let the music play through them. This illustrates the difference between serving God as slaves and living as mature sons. The Mirror Bible expresses this reality in Galatians 4:7: "Therefore you are no longer a slave but a son, and if a son, then an heir of God through Christ."

Consider how this transforms everything. Mature sons don't serve God to earn approval—they serve from approval. They don't work for inheritance—they work from inheritance. They don't strive for victory—they live from victory. The Passion Translation captures this shift in Romans 8:15: "And you did not receive the 'spirit of religious duty,' leading you back into the fear of never being good enough. But you have received the 'Spirit of full acceptance,' enfolding you into the family of God."

Let me share a story that illuminates this truth. A father took his young son to their family business for the first time. The son asked, "Dad, what do I need to do to earn my place here?" The father smiled and said, "Son, you don't need to earn your place—you're my son. This place is already yours. Now, let me teach you how to steward what's already yours." This perfectly illustrates how mature sons operate—not from earning but from owning.

Think about how a tree bears fruit. It doesn't strain or struggle—it simply manifests what's already in its nature. The Mirror Bible illuminates this natural expression in John 15:5: "I am the vine, you are the branches. He who abides in Me, and I in him, bears much fruit; for without Me you can do nothing." Mature sons understand that fruitfulness flows from connection, not effort.

The early church father Irenaeus wrote, "The glory of God is man fully alive." This "fully alive" state is mature sonship—living naturally from our true identity. The Passion Translation renders

John 10:10: "I have come to give you everything in abundance, more than you expect—life in its fullness until you overflow!"

Practical Expressions of Mature Sonship

Begin each day from inheritance, not toward it. The Mirror Bible reminds us in Ephesians 1:3: "Blessed be the God and Father of our Lord Jesus Christ, who has blessed us with every spiritual blessing in the heavenly places in Christ." Notice the past tense—has blessed, not will bless.

Face challenges as an owner, not a victim. Like Joshua and Caleb who saw the Promised Land as already theirs, mature sons see challenges through inheritance eyes. The Mirror Bible expresses this in Romans 8:37: "In all these things we are super conquerors through him who loved us!"

Let work flow from rest, not toward it. Mature sons understand the paradox that true productivity flows from rest in identity, not striving for identity. The Passion Translation illuminates this in Hebrews 4:3: "For we who believe enter into the realm of rest."

Build relationships from fullness, not need. When we know we're complete in Christ, we can give freely without demanding anything in return. The Mirror Bible captures this in 1 John 4:19: "We love because he first loved us."

Create from sonship, not toward it. Like an artist who creates not to become an artist but because they are one, mature sons express life naturally from their identity. The Mirror Bible expresses this in Ephesians 2:10: "We are his poetry, we are the words of his story."

Chapter Summary

The journey from slavery to sonship follows a divine pattern: liberation from Egypt (slave identity), wilderness training (mindset transformation), Jordan crossing (inheritance consciousness), facing giants (manifesting sonship), and living as mature sons (natural expression of divine life). This isn't just ancient history—it's the map for our own transformation from religious slaves to mature sons who naturally express divine life. Like Israel's journey to the Promised Land, each stage is essential for our development, moving us from merely knowing about our inheritance to actually living from it. Just as Egypt's slave mentality had to die in the wilderness before Israel could enter their inheritance, we too must shed old mindsets and identities to fully step into mature sonship. This pattern isn't about achieving something new but about progressively awakening to and manifesting what's already true—our identity as sons and daughters who naturally carry and express divine life.

Reflection Questions

1. Where in your life are you still operating from slave consciousness rather than son consciousness?

2. How might your approach to challenges change if you viewed them through inheritance eyes?

3. What areas of your life need to shift from striving toward sonship to living from sonship?

4. How could your relationships transform if you lived consistently as a mature son?

5. What practical steps can you take to begin living more fully from your inheritance rather than toward it?

Chapter 7

Breaking Free from False Identity

The Journey to Authentic Self

In the heart of the Amazon rainforest grows a fascinating plant called the strangler fig. It begins life as a tiny seed deposited high in a host tree's branches. As it grows, it sends roots down around the host tree, eventually creating a lattice-like network that completely encases the original tree. Over time, the host tree dies and rots away, leaving only the hollow fig tree—an outer structure that looks like a tree but is actually just a shell of the original. This natural phenomenon perfectly illustrates how false identity works—it grows around our true identity, creating an elaborate structure that appears to be who we are but is actually a construct that strangles our true nature.

In today's world, people typically build their identity on shifting foundations: their job titles, career achievements, family standing, or others' opinions. 'I'm a doctor,' 'I'm a CEO,' 'I'm from a poor family,' 'I'm not as successful as my siblings'—these role-based and comparison-based identities create a veneer that obscures their true nature. The Mirror Bible expresses this tragedy in John 1:11-12: 'He came to his own people, but they didn't receive him. But those who did receive him, he gave them the authority to become children of God!'

Even many believers find it difficult to truly embrace their identity as sons and daughters of God, despite scripture declaring this truth repeatedly. They might mentally assent to being God's children, yet continue living from lesser identities. Like someone born into royalty but raised by peasants, they cannot imagine themselves as divine offspring. This stunted vision leads to stunted living. The

Passion Translation captures this in 1 John 3:1-2: 'Look with wonder at the depth of the Father's marvelous love that he has lavished on us! He has called us and made us his very own children... Beloved, we are God's children right now!'"

The Mirror Bible illuminates this reality in 2 Corinthians 5:16-17: "From now on we recognize no one according to their actions or appearance... In Christ, every person discovers their true identity! The old is gone; look—what has become new is of the essence of God!" Breaking free from false identity begins with recognizing that what we've thought of as "me" might actually be a construct that's grown around our true identity in Christ.

Jesus told a profound story that perfectly captures this struggle with false identity—the parable of the two sons (traditionally called the prodigal son story). The Passion Translation renders Luke 15:11: "There was once a father who had two sons." Notice that both sons were sons from the beginning—their sonship wasn't in question. What was in question was their consciousness of their true identity.

Think about how a frozen river works. The surface might be solid ice, but beneath that frozen layer, the real river continues to flow. Similarly, beneath all our false identities, our true identity in Christ continues to flow, waiting to be rediscovered. The early church father Gregory of Nyssa described this as "removing the coverings that have grown around the image of God within us."

Understanding False Identity

In the world of computer programming, there's a concept called "technical debt"—layers of temporary fixes and workarounds that accumulate over time until they become part of the system's structure. While these patches might have served a purpose initially, they eventually create a complex maze that obscures the original code. Our false identities work similarly—they're layers of adaptations and coping mechanisms that, over time, become so familiar we mistake them for our true selves.

The Mirror Bible expresses this layering effect in Colossians 3:9-10: "Do not lie to one another, since you have stripped off the old self with its practices and have put on the new self, which is being renewed in knowledge according to the image of the one who created it." Notice the language—"stripped off" suggests these false identities are like garments we've worn so long we've forgotten they're not our skin.

Consider how pearls form. When an irritant enters an oyster's shell, the oyster covers it with layer after layer of nacre as a defense mechanism. Similarly, our false identities often begin as protection against pain, disappointment, or fear. The Passion Translation illuminates this in 2 Corinthians 3:15-16: "When the Scripture is read, it seems as though Moses' veil hangs over their minds, shadowing their understanding. But the moment one turns to the Lord with an open heart, the veil is lifted and they see."

Let me share a story that illustrates this truth. A gifted artist struggled for years with perfectionism that paralyzed her creativity. During therapy, she discovered that this perfectionism began in childhood when her art was criticized. What started as protection against hurt became a prison that kept her from expressing her true gift. The Mirror Bible captures this dynamic in 2 Corinthians 3:17: "Now the Lord is the Spirit, and where the Spirit of the Lord is, there is freedom."

False Identity often manifests in three primary patterns:

The Achievement Identity: Like the elder son in Jesus' parable, this false self builds identity on performance and moral superiority. The Mirror Bible expresses its trap in Galatians 3:3: "Are you so foolish? Having begun by the Spirit, are you now being perfected by the flesh?" This identity measures worth by accomplishments rather than acceptance.

The Rebellion Identity: Like the younger son initially, this false self defines itself by what it's against. The Passion Translation captures this in Romans 7:15: "I'm a mystery to myself, for I want to do what is right, but end up doing what my moral instincts condemn." This identity seeks freedom through resistance rather than relationship.

The Adaptation Identity: This false self shapes itself to meet others' expectations. The early church father Irenaeus described this as "wearing a mask that doesn't belong to us." This identity seeks safety through conformity rather than authenticity.

Think about how method actors prepare for roles. They can become so immersed in a character that they temporarily lose touch with their true identity. The Mirror Bible illuminates this danger in 2 Corinthians 10:12: "We dare not classify or compare ourselves with some who commend themselves. When they measure themselves by themselves and compare themselves with themselves, they are without understanding."

False identity also manifests in what psychologists call "compensatory behaviors"—attempts to prove or disprove the false self's claims. Like a hamster wheel, these behaviors keep us busy but never lead to true rest. The Passion Translation expresses this futility in Matthew 11:28: "Are you weary, carrying a heavy burden? Come to me. I will refresh your life, for I am your oasis."

Consider how different this is from true identity. False identity must be maintained through constant effort, like spinning plates that will crash if we stop spinning them. True identity, by contrast, is like gravity—it's simply there, requiring no effort to maintain. The Mirror Bible captures this in Colossians 2:10: "And you are complete in Him, who is the head of all principality and power."

The Two Sons' Delusion

Jesus' parable of the two sons offers us perhaps the most profound exploration of false identity ever told. Like two sides of the same coin, each son represents a different manifestation of the same fundamental delusion—that sonship is something to be earned rather than received. The Mirror Bible illuminates this in Luke

15:29 and 15:19, where both sons use the language of servants rather than sons: "Look, these many years I have served you" (elder) and "Make me like one of your hired servants" (younger).

Consider how a prismatic crystal splits pure light into different colours. Similarly, the father's pure love reveals different forms of false identity in each son. The Passion Translation captures the elder son's reaction in Luke 15:29: "All these years I've served you, and I've never once disobeyed any of your commands. Yet you've never thrown me a party..." His inherited sonship had devolved into earned servanthood.

Let me share a story that illustrates this truth. Two brothers inherited their father's successful business. The older brother worked tirelessly, measuring his worth by his contribution to the company. The younger brother rebelled, starting rival ventures that failed. Years later, in therapy, they realized both were trying to prove something—one through achievement, one through independence. Neither could simply receive their inheritance as sons. The Mirror Bible expresses this common root in Galatians 4:7: "Therefore you are no longer a slave but a son, and if a son, then an heir of God through Christ."

Think about how a tree grows. If its trunk is bent when young, it will grow in compensating patterns that become more elaborate over time. The elder son's false identity grew in patterns of performance and moral superiority. The younger son's grew in patterns of rebellion and self-destruction. Yet both patterns stemmed from the same root—disconnection from their true identity as sons.

The elder son's delusion manifested in several ways:
- Measuring love by performance: "These many years I have served you"
- Keeping moral scorecard: "I never disobeyed your command"
- Comparing with others: "This son of yours who devoured your property"

- Living from duty rather than delight: "All these years I've worked like a slave"

The younger son's delusion showed different symptoms:
- Seeking identity through independence: "Give me my share"
- Defining freedom as absence of relationship: "Traveled to a distant country"
- Trying to earn what was freely given: "Make me like a hired servant"
- Believing distance could separate him from sonship: "I am no longer worthy"

The early church father Augustine noted how both sons sought to create their own identity apart from the father's love—one through moral achievement, the other through moral failure. The Passion Translation captures this mutual delusion in Romans 8:15: "And you did not receive the 'spirit of religious duty,' leading you back into the fear of never being good enough."

Consider how different this is from the father's perspective. When the younger son was still far off, the father ran to him—something considered undignified for eastern patriarchs. When the elder son refused to join the celebration, the father went out to him. The Mirror Bible expresses this persistent love in 1 John 4:19: "We love because he first loved us."

Even more revealing is what the sons couldn't see about themselves. The elder son didn't realize he was as far from the father's heart in the fields as his brother had been in the far country. The younger son didn't realize he was as much a son in the pigpen as he had been in the father's house. The Passion Translation illuminates this blindness in 2 Corinthians 3:16: "But the moment one turns to the Lord with an open heart, the veil is lifted and they see."

Recognizing the True Self

In the world of art restoration, experts sometimes discover masterpieces hidden beneath layers of later paintings. Using advanced imaging technology, they can see the original work before beginning the delicate process of removal. Similarly, recognizing our true self requires first seeing what's authentic beneath the layers of false identity we've accumulated. The Mirror Bible expresses this reality in 2 Corinthians 3:18: "In him, every face mirrors the glory of the Lord. We are transfigured by the Spirit of the Lord in our constant beholding, from glory to glory."

Consider how a diamond forms. Deep in the earth, under intense pressure and heat, carbon atoms align themselves into a crystal structure that becomes one of the most brilliant substances in nature. The pressure doesn't create the diamond—it reveals what was always potentially present in the carbon. The Passion Translation captures this transformative process in 2 Corinthians 4:7: "We are like common clay jars that carry this glorious treasure within, so that the extraordinary overflow of power will be seen as God's, not ours."

Let me share a story that illuminates this truth. A renowned violin maker was known for his ability to create instruments of exceptional quality. When asked his secret, he said, "I don't create the music in the wood—I release it. Every piece of wood has its own song. My job is to remove everything that isn't that song." The Mirror Bible reflects this principle in Colossians 3:3-4: "Your life is now hidden with Christ in God. Christ is your life!"

The early church fathers described true self-recognition as "remembering who we are." Like someone waking from a dream, we don't create a new identity—we remember our original one. The Passion Translation renders Ephesians 5:14: "Awake, O sleeper, rise up from the dead, and Christ will shine his light into you!"
Think about how a GPS system works. It doesn't just show where you are—it constantly compares your current position with your true destination.

Recognition of true self works similarly. The Mirror Bible expresses this in Philippians 3:12: "Not that I have already obtained all this, or have already arrived at my goal, but I press on to take hold of that for which Christ Jesus took hold of me."

Let me share a remarkable story from South Africa's Kruger National Park that captures this truth about breaking free from false identity. An eagle had been kept in captivity for many years, confined to a zoo enclosure that limited its movements and horizon. When the authorities finally decided to release it back to the wild, they carefully transported it to an ideal location and opened its cage. But something unexpected happened—the eagle didn't fly. Years of confinement had conditioned it to live beneath its true nature. It remained earthbound, having forgotten its capacity to soar.

This continued until one day, the eagle caught sight of another eagle soaring high above. Something awakened in that moment—seeing one of its own kind flying free triggered a recognition of its true nature. In that instant, the eagle remembered who it really was, spread its wings, and took to the skies, soaring as it was always meant to.

This powerfully illustrates our journey of breaking free from false identity. Like that eagle, many of us have been confined by limiting beliefs, others' expectations, and false self-images. We've grown accustomed to living far below our true nature. But when we catch a glimpse of Christ in us—when we see our true nature reflected in Him—something awakens. The Mirror Bible expresses this transformative awakening in 2 Corinthians 3:18: 'We can all draw close to him with the veil removed from our faces. And with no veil we all become like mirrors who brightly reflect the glory of the Lord Jesus.'

Key markers of the true self include:

1. *Natural Flow vs. Forced Effort.* The true self flows naturally, like water finding its path. False identity

requires constant maintenance. The Passion Translation captures this in Matthew 11:29-30: "Simply join your life with mine... Learn the unforced rhythms of grace."

2. *Rest vs. Striving.* True identity operates from rest, while false identity constantly strives to prove itself. The Mirror Bible illuminates this in Hebrews 4:3: "We who believe enter that rest."

3. *Giving vs. Getting.* The true self naturally gives because it knows its fullness. False identity constantly takes because it feels empty. The Mirror Bible expresses this in Acts 20:35: "There is more happiness in giving than in receiving."

4. *Being vs. Doing.* True identity flows from being, while false identity depends on doing. The Passion Translation renders John 7:38: "The one who believes in me... from within him will flow rivers of living water."

5. *Present vs. Past/Future.* The true self lives in the now, while false identity constantly references past achievements or future goals. The Mirror Bible captures this in 2 Corinthians 6:2: "Now is the time of God's favor, now is the day of salvation."

Breaking Free from False Patterns

In the mountains of Japan, there's an ancient art called kintsugi—repairing broken pottery with gold. Instead of hiding the breaks, the gold lines celebrate them, creating something more beautiful than the original. This art perfectly illustrates how breaking free from false patterns isn't about hiding our brokenness but about letting divine life shine through our authentic journey. The Mirror Bible expresses this transformation in 2 Corinthians 4:7: "We have this treasure in earthen vessels, that the excellency of the power may be of God, and not of us."

Consider how a caterpillar transforms into a butterfly. The process isn't just about growing wings—it requires the complete dissolution of the caterpillar's former identity. Inside the chrysalis, the caterpillar literally liquefies before reforming as a butterfly. The Passion Translation captures this radical transformation in 2 Corinthians 5:17: "Now, if anyone is enfolded into Christ, he has become an entirely new creation. All that is related to the old order has vanished. Behold, everything is fresh and new."

Let me share a story that illuminates this truth. A master potter was teaching his apprentice about centering clay on the wheel. The apprentice kept trying to force the clay into position. The master stopped him and said, "Your problem isn't with the clay—it's with your grip. You're holding so tightly that you can't feel when the clay is actually centered. Loosen your grip and let your hands sense the clay's true center." This perfectly illustrates how breaking free from false patterns often requires letting go rather than trying harder.

The early church fathers saw this process as "detachment"—not in the sense of becoming cold or distant, but in the sense of releasing our grip on false identities. The Mirror Bible illuminates this in Colossians 3:9-10: "Do not lie to one another, since you have stripped off the old self with its practices and have put on the new self."

Think about how a skilled surgeon removes scar tissue. They don't attack the scar directly—they work with the body's natural healing processes to release the adhesions that restrict movement. Similarly, breaking free from false patterns isn't about attacking them but about releasing their hold through alignment with our true nature. The Passion Translation expresses this in Romans 12:2: "Stop imitating the ideals and opinions of the culture around you, but be inwardly transformed by the Holy Spirit through a total reformation of how you think."

Practical steps for breaking free:

1. *Recognition Without Reaction.* When false patterns arise, recognize them without fighting them. The Mirror Bible captures this awareness in 2 Corinthians 3:16: "The moment one turns to face the Lord the veil is lifted."

2. *Return to Rest.* Instead of struggling with false patterns, return to the rest of true identity. The Passion Translation renders Matthew 11:28: "Are you weary, carrying a heavy burden? Come to me. I will refresh your life, for I am your oasis."

3. *Release Through Remembrance.* Release false patterns by remembering who you truly are. The Mirror Bible expresses this in Colossians 3:3: "Your life is now hidden with Christ in God."

4. *Realign with Truth.* Let every circumstance become an opportunity to realign with true identity. The Mirror Bible guides us in 2 Corinthians 10:5: "We capture every thought and make it give up and obey Christ."

5. *Respond from Reality.* Instead of reacting from false patterns, respond from true identity. The Passion Translation illuminates this in 1 John 4:17: "As he is, so are we in this world."

Even our "failures" in this process become opportunities for greater awareness. Like a martial artist who learns more from falling than from staying upright, our struggles with false patterns can deepen our recognition of true identity. The Mirror Bible captures this redemptive perspective in Romans 8:28: "Meanwhile we know that the love of God causes everything to mutually contribute to our advantage."

Living from True Identity

In the heart of ancient redwood forests, scientists have discovered something remarkable. These massive trees don't survive through deep individual root systems but through interconnected roots that form a vast underground network. Each tree lives not as an isolated entity but as part of a greater whole. This natural phenomenon perfectly illustrates living from true identity—not as separate selves striving to survive, but as expressions of one divine life. The Mirror Bible captures this reality in John 15:5: "I am the vine, you are the branches. Those who remain in me, and I in them, will produce much fruit. For apart from me you can do nothing."

Think about how a master dancer moves. After years of training, they no longer think about the steps—they simply express the music flowing through them. The Passion Translation illuminates this natural expression in Galatians 2:20: "My old identity has been co-crucified with Messiah and no longer lives... and the life I now live in this body, I live by the faith of the Son of God."

Let me share a story that illuminates this truth. A young musician was struggling with stage fright before performances. His teacher shared a profound insight: "Your fear comes from thinking about yourself—how you'll perform, what others will think. Instead, become a servant of the music. When you live to express the music rather than prove yourself, fear dissolves into flow." This perfectly illustrates how living from true identity dissolves the anxiety of false self-consciousness.

The early church father Gregory of Nyssa described this as "eternal progress in God"—not a destination we reach but a life we live from. The Mirror Bible expresses this journey in 2 Corinthians 3:18: "We are transfigured by the Spirit of the Lord in our constant beholding, from glory to glory."

Living from true identity manifests in several ways:

1. *Natural Expression vs. Forced Performance*. True identity flows like a river finding its natural course. The Passion Translation renders John 7:38: "Rivers of living water will flow from within them." We don't have to force the flow—we align with it.

2. *Present-Moment Awareness*. Living from true identity happens in the now. The Mirror Bible captures this in 2 Corinthians 6:2: "Now is the time of God's favor, now is the day of salvation." False identity constantly references past or future, but true identity lives in the eternal now.

3. *Authentic Relationships*. When we live from true identity, relationships become expressions of love rather than attempts to get love. The Mirror Bible illuminates this in 1 John 4:19: "We love because he first loved us."

4. *Creative Freedom*. True identity naturally creates from fullness rather than lack. The Passion Translation expresses this in Ephesians 2:10: "We have become his poetry, a re-created people that will fulfill the destiny he has given each of us."

5. *Restful Activity*. Like a bird soaring on thermal currents, we learn to work from rest rather than striving. The Mirror Bible renders Hebrews 4:3: "We who believe enter that rest."

Consider how light travels through space. It doesn't effort its way forward—it simply expresses its nature. Similarly, living from true identity isn't about trying to become something but expressing what we already are. The early church father Irenaeus expressed this as "the glory of God is a human being fully alive."

Practical Expressions for Daily Life

Begin each day from identity rather than toward it. The Mirror Bible reminds us in Colossians 3:4: "Christ is your life!" This isn't a goal to achieve but a reality to live from.

Face challenges from wholeness rather than lack. The Passion Translation captures this in Philippians 4:13: "I find the strength to face all conditions by the power that Christ gives me."

Let work flow from being rather than doing. Instead of working to become something, let your work express who you already are. The Mirror Bible expresses this in Ephesians 2:10: "We are his poetry."

Build relationships from fullness rather than need. When we know we're complete in Christ, we can give freely without demanding anything in return. The Mirror Bible illuminates this in 1 John 4:16: "God is love, and all who live in love live in God, and God lives in them."

Chapter Summary

Breaking free from false identity isn't about creating a new self but discovering our true self in Christ. Like removing layers that have grown around our authentic identity, this process involves recognition, release, and realignment with truth. As we learn to live from true identity rather than false patterns, we naturally express divine life through our unique personality and circumstances. Just as a sculptor removes excess stone to reveal the masterpiece within, this journey isn't about adding something new but uncovering what's always been true. Each false identity—whether rooted in past experiences, religious conditioning, or cultural programming—falls away as we awaken to who we've always been in Christ. This transformation isn't achieved through struggle but through growing awareness of our true nature, allowing divine life to naturally express itself as these false layers dissolve in the light of truth.

Reflection Questions

1. How might your daily life change if you consistently lived from true identity rather than false patterns?

2. What aspects of false identity still feel "safer" than living from your true self in Christ?

3. How could your relationships transform if you lived consistently from wholeness rather than need?

4. What practical steps can you take to maintain awareness of your true identity throughout the day?

5. How might your work change if it flowed from being rather than doing?

Chapter 8
Placement as Mature Sons

Beyond Traditional Adoption

In ancient Rome, there existed a profound ceremony called "*toga virilis*"—the coming of age ritual where a youth was formally recognized as a mature son, capable of representing the family's interests. This wasn't about making someone a son who wasn't one before—it was about recognizing and placing a natural son in the position of mature sonship. This ancient practice illuminates the true meaning of what scripture calls "*huiothesia*," often mistranslated simply as "adoption."

The Mirror Bible captures this reality in Galatians 4:1-2: "Let me explain: as long as an heir is a minor, he is no better off than a slave, even though he is the legal owner of the estate. He still has to listen to guardians and trustees until he reaches the age set by his father." Notice carefully—the heir was always a son; what changed was his placement into the position of mature sonship.

Consider how different this is from our modern understanding of adoption. The Passion Translation illuminates this distinction in Ephesians 1:5: "For it was always in his perfect plan to adopt us as his delightful children, through our union with Jesus, the Anointed One." The Greek word huiothesia doesn't mean bringing an outsider into the family—it means placing a son who is already in the family into the position of mature sonship.

Think about how a master craftsman trains an apprentice. The training isn't about making the apprentice part of the craft—it's about bringing them into the full expression of what they're already part of. The early church father Athanasius expressed this when he wrote, "God became what we are so that we might become what He is." This isn't about changing our essential nature but about manifesting our true nature in Christ.

Understanding Huiothesia

In the world of classical music, there's a profound distinction between being a student and being recognized as a master. A student at the conservatory might have all the necessary skills, but there comes a moment of formal recognition—often through a debut performance—where they're acknowledged as a master in their own right. This isn't about becoming something they weren't before; it's about being placed in the position their training has prepared them for. This perfectly illustrates the concept of huiothesia.

The Mirror Bible illuminates this reality in Romans 8:15: "The Spirit you received does not make you slaves, so that you live in fear again; rather, the Spirit you received brought about your huiothesia." Notice that the Spirit doesn't make us sons—He places us as sons who can function in mature sonship.

Let me share a story that captures this truth. In a traditional Japanese pottery family, the son of the master potter had been training since childhood. Though he was always the master's son, there came a ceremonial moment when his father formally recognized him as a master potter in his own right, entrusting him with the family's secret glazing techniques and giving him authority to sign works with the family seal. This wasn't about making him part of the family—he was born into that. It was about placing him in the position of mature responsibility and authority.

The early church fathers understood huiothesia as placement into the full rights and responsibilities of sonship. The Passion Translation expresses this in Galatians 4:4-5: "But when the time of fulfilment had come, God sent his Son... to purchase our freedom and to set us free from the law's demands—so that we would be given our full status as sons."

Think about how a prince becomes king. The prince is always the king's son by birth, but there comes a coronation moment where he's formally placed in the position his birth destined him for. The Mirror Bible captures this progression in 1 John 3:2: "Beloved, we are God's children now, and what we will be has not yet appeared; but we know that when he appears we shall be like him, because we shall see him as he is."

Huiothesia involves several key elements:

Recognition of Identity: Like a DNA test confirming parentage, huiothesia formally recognizes what was always true. The Mirror Bible expresses this in Galatians 4:6: "And because we are his true sons, God has released the Spirit of his Son into our hearts, who now lives in us."

Authorization for Representation: Just as a company executive receives authority to act on behalf of the company, huiothesia includes authority to represent the Father. The Passion Translation illuminates this in John 20:21: "As the Father has sent me, so I send you."

Access to Resources: Similar to a son receiving access to family business accounts, huiothesia includes access to all the Father's resources. The Mirror Bible renders Ephesians 1:3: "Blessed be the God and Father of our Lord Jesus Christ, who has blessed us with every spiritual blessing in the heavenly places in Christ."

Assignment of Responsibility: Like a craft master entrusting their techniques to an apprentice, huiothesia includes responsibility to steward and extend the family heritage. The Passion Translation captures this in 2 Corinthians 5:20: "We are ambassadors of the Anointed One who carry the message of Christ to the world."

From Children to Mature Sons

In the highlands of Scotland grows a remarkable tree—the Fortingall Yew. What appears to be several separate trees is actually one ancient being that has grown for over 3,000 years, maturing from a single sapling into a vast, interconnected system. This natural progression illustrates our journey from spiritual children to mature sons—not becoming something different, but growing into the fullness of what we already are. The Mirror Bible expresses this reality in Galatians 4:1-2: "As long as the heir is a child, he does not differ from a slave, though he is owner of everything."

Consider how Jesus Himself progressed in His human experience. The Passion Translation captures this in Luke 2:52: "And Jesus grew in wisdom and stature, and in favor with God and man." This wasn't about becoming more divine—He was fully divine from conception. It was about bringing His human consciousness into alignment with His true identity.

Let me share a story that illuminates this truth. A master violinist was watching his young son practice. The boy, frustrated with a difficult passage, exclaimed, "I'll never be as good as you!" The father smiled and said, "You already have the same music in you that I have. The difference isn't in the music—it's in the awareness of it. My playing isn't about becoming musical; it's about letting the music that's already there flow freely." This perfectly illustrates our progression from children to mature sons.

The early church father Irenaeus described this progression using the metaphor of fruit ripening. Just as an unripe fruit isn't less of a fruit—it simply hasn't reached its full expression—so spiritual children aren't less sons; they're simply growing into full expression. The Mirror Bible illuminates this in Ephesians 4:13: "Until we all reach unity in the faith and in the knowledge of the Son of God and become mature, attaining to the whole measure of the fullness of Christ."

Think about how a masterpiece emerges from a block of marble. The sculptor doesn't add anything to the marble—they remove what obscures the form within. Similarly, our progression to mature sonship isn't about adding something to us but about removing what blocks the expression of who we already are. The Passion Translation renders 2 Corinthians 3:18: "We can all draw close to him with the veil removed from our faces. And with no veil we all become like mirrors who brightly reflect the glory of the Lord Jesus."

The Stages of Maturity

Within our journey from children to mature sons, scripture reveals distinct stages of development. The Greek language captures these nuances that English translations often miss. Like a seed progressing through definite stages to become a fruit-bearing tree, our spiritual development follows a divine pattern:

Nepios (Infant): The beginning stage where one is unable to speak or fully express divine life. The Mirror Bible captures this stage in 1 Corinthians 13:11: "When I was a nepios (infant), I spoke as an infant, I understood as an infant, I thought as an infant."

Paidion (Young Child): The stage of early development and basic learning. The Passion Translation expresses this in 1 John 2:13: "I am writing to you, little children (paidion), because you know the Father."

Teknon (Child/Born One): One who shares the family nature but is still growing in expression. The Mirror Bible illuminates this in Romans 8:16: "The Spirit himself testifies with our spirit that we are teknon (born ones) of God."

Huios (Mature Son): The fully developed son who can represent family interests. The Passion Translation renders Galatians 4:7: "Now you are no longer a slave but God's own huios (mature son)."

Jesus Himself demonstrated this progression in His human experience. Luke 2:40, 52 tells us that He "grew in wisdom and stature, and in favor with God and man." Though He was always the eternal Son, in His humanity He modeled the perfect pattern of development from infant to mature son. This wasn't about becoming more divine—He was fully divine from conception. Rather, it was about His human consciousness aligning with and expressing His true identity in increasing measure.

Responsibility Growth: Just as a young heir progressively takes on more family responsibilities, we grow in our ability to represent the Father. The Passion Translation captures this in 2 Corinthians 5:20: "We are ambassadors of the Anointed One."

Authority Expression: Like a prince learning to exercise royal authority appropriately, we learn to move in spiritual authority. The Mirror Bible illuminates this in Luke 10:19: "Behold, I give unto you power... over all the power of the enemy."

Character Development: Just as precious metal is refined by fire, our character aligns with our identity through life experiences. The Passion Translation renders James 1:4: "Let perseverance finish its work so that you may be mature and complete, not lacking anything."

The Position of Maturity

In the world of quantum physics, there's a fascinating phenomenon called "quantum entanglement" where two particles, once connected, remain instantaneously linked regardless of distance. What happens to one immediately affects the other. This offers us a picture of mature sonship—so aligned with the Father's nature that His life naturally expresses through us. The Mirror Bible captures this reality in 1 John 4:17: "The same love that he is, we are in this world!"

Consider how a master craftsman eventually becomes one with their craft. There's no separation between the craftsman and their work—the work is simply an expression of who they are. The Passion Translation illuminates this unity in Galatians 2:20: "And now the essence of this new life is no longer mine, for the Anointed One lives his life through me—we live in union as one!"

Let me share a story that illustrates this truth. A renowned conductor was asked how he achieved such perfect synchronization with his orchestra. He replied, "There comes a point where I'm not conducting the music—I am the music, and so are they. We're not following each other; we're expressing the same reality together." This perfectly captures the position of mature sonship—complete alignment with divine nature.

The early church father Maximus the Confessor described this position as "natural movement according to nature." Like a river naturally flowing according to its nature, mature sons naturally express divine life. The Mirror Bible expresses this in Colossians 2:9-10: "For in Christ all the fullness of Deity lives in bodily form, and in Christ you have been brought to fullness."

Think about how a hologram works. Unlike a photograph, every piece of a hologram contains the whole image. Similarly, mature sons carry and express the whole nature of God, not just parts. The Passion Translation renders Ephesians 3:19: "Then you will be empowered to discover what every holy one experiences—the great magnitude of the astonishing love of Christ in all its dimensions."

Characteristics of the Position of Maturity:

Complete Alignment: Like a master dancer who becomes one with the music, mature sons move in perfect harmony with divine nature. The Mirror Bible illuminates this in John 5:19: "The Son can do nothing by himself; he can only do what he sees his Father doing."

Natural Authority: Similar to how a seasoned pilot naturally responds to changing conditions, mature sons exercise authority without strain or effort. The Passion Translation captures this in

Mark 11:23: "For assuredly, I say to you, whoever says to this mountain, 'Be removed and be cast into the sea,' and does not doubt in his heart..."

Intuitive Wisdom: Like a master chess player who sees moves intuitively, mature sons naturally know the Father's ways. The Mirror Bible expresses this in 1 Corinthians 2:16: "For who has known the mind of the Lord that he may instruct Him? But we have the mind of Christ."

Representative Capacity: Just as an ambassador naturally represents their country, mature sons naturally represent the Father. The Passion Translation renders 2 Corinthians 5:20: "We are ambassadors of the Anointed One who carry the message of Christ to the world."

Family Authority and Responsibility

In the natural world, there exists a remarkable phenomenon known as *mycelial* networks—vast underground systems of fungal threads that connect entire forests, sharing resources and information. Scientists call these networks the "Wood Wide Web." Individual trees, while maintaining their distinct identity, operate as part of this larger family system. This natural wonder illustrates how mature sons function—exercising individual authority while maintaining perfect family harmony. The Mirror Bible expresses this reality in John 15:5: "I am the vine, you are the branches. Those who remain in me, and I in them, will produce much fruit."

Consider how a symphony orchestra works at its highest level. Each musician exercises individual authority over their instrument while maintaining perfect harmony with the whole. The Passion Translation captures this divine harmony in 1 Corinthians 12:27: "You are the body of Christ and each one of you is a vital part of it."

Let me share a story that illuminates this truth. A father owned a vast business enterprise. When his son reached maturity, he didn't just give him authority—he taught him the family way of doing business. "Our authority," he explained, "isn't about power over others—it's about empowering others. That's the family character." This perfectly illustrates how mature sons exercise authority—not through dominance but through the Father's nature of self-giving love.

The early church father Gregory of Nyssa described this as "movement according to nature." Just as planets naturally move according to both their individual orbits and the larger gravitational harmony, mature sons exercise authority in perfect alignment with family nature. The Mirror Bible illuminates this in Philippians 2:5-7: "Let this mind be in you which was also in Christ Jesus, who... made himself of no reputation, taking the form of a bondservant."

Think about how a master martial artist operates. Their authority doesn't come from force but from such perfect alignment with natural principles that power flows effortlessly. The Passion Translation renders Matthew 8:9: "For I am under authority, and I have authority over others... I say to one, 'Go,' and he goes, and to another, 'Come,' and he comes."

Key Aspects of Family Authority:

Alignment Before Action: Like a pilot who checks their instruments before takeoff, mature sons align with family nature before exercising authority. The Mirror Bible expresses this in John 5:19: "The Son can do nothing of Himself, but what He sees the Father do."

Character-Based Authority: Similar to how a judge's authority comes from representing the law rather than personal power, mature sons exercise authority from family character. The Passion Translation captures this in 2 Corinthians 10:8: "Our authority is for building you up, not for tearing you down."

Responsibility to Empower: Just as a healthy parent empowers their children rather than controlling them, mature sons use authority to release others into their inheritance. The Mirror Bible illuminates this in Ephesians 4:12: "To equip the saints for the work of ministry, for building up the body of Christ."

Family Representation: Like an ambassador whose authority comes from perfectly representing their nation, mature sons carry authority through accurate representation of family nature. The Passion Translation renders 2 Corinthians 5:20: "We are ambassadors of the Anointed One who carry the message of Christ to the world."

Living as Placed Sons

In the world of classical ballet, there's a profound moment called "placement"—the perfect alignment of body, balance, and movement that allows complex choreography to flow naturally. Once a dancer finds true placement, what seemed difficult becomes effortless. Similarly, living as placed sons isn't about constant effort but about maintaining alignment with our true position. The Mirror Bible expresses this reality in Colossians 2:6-7: "As you have received Christ Jesus the Lord, so walk in Him, rooted and built up in Him and established in the faith."

Consider how a master surfer rides waves. They're not fighting the ocean's power but aligning with it so perfectly that they become one with its movement. The Passion Translation captures this flow in Galatians 5:25: "If we live by the Spirit, let us also walk by the Spirit."

Let me share a story that illuminates this truth. A tea master was teaching his student about the perfect pour. The student was trying too hard, focusing on every movement. The master said, "Stop trying to pour the tea—let the tea pour itself through you. When you find true placement, you disappear and only the tea remains." This perfectly illustrates how placed sons live—not through effort but through perfect alignment that allows divine life to flow naturally.

The early church father Maximus the Confessor described this as "natural movement according to nature." Like a river that doesn't strain to flow—it simply moves according to its nature—placed sons naturally express divine life. The Mirror Bible illuminates this in 1 John 4:17: "As he is, so are we in this world!"

Consider how fundamentally identity shapes perception and behavior. When someone realizes they belong to royalty, everything changes—not just their circumstances but their entire way of being. A person who knows they are of royal blood carries themselves differently. They don't struggle with feelings of inferiority, lack, or fear. They naturally walk with confidence, know they have access to kingdom resources, and operate from a place of security. The Mirror Bible expresses this royal consciousness in 1 Peter 2:9: 'You are a chosen people, a royal priesthood, a holy nation, God's special possession.'

This is not about pride but about accurate self-perception. Like a prince who finally discovers his true heritage, mature sons live from the unshakeable knowledge of their royal identity in Christ. The Passion Translation captures this reality in Romans 8:17: 'And since we are his true children, we qualify to share all his treasures, for indeed, we are heirs of God himself.' This inheritance consciousness transforms everything—how we think, how we speak, how we act, how we face challenges.

Practical Expressions and Signs

Like a master craftsman who works with effortless expertise, placed sons naturally express divine life through every aspect of living. The early church fathers called this state "second nature"—when divine life becomes so natural it flows without conscious effort.

Begin Each Day from Position: Like a compass that naturally points north, start each day aligned with your true position in Christ. The Mirror Bible expresses this in Colossians 3:1: "Since, then, you have been raised with Christ, set your hearts on things above."

Face Challenges from Rest: Instead of reacting to circumstances, respond from your position of rest as a placed son. Even in intense activity, there's an underlying peace that comes from secure placement. The Mirror Bible captures this in Hebrews 4:3: "We who have believed enter that rest."

Exercise Natural Authority: Like a seasoned captain navigating through storms, authority flows naturally from your placement rather than through effort. The Mirror Bible expresses this in Luke 10:19: "Behold, I give you authority..."

Build Relationships from Family Position: Just as a secure heir naturally gives rather than takes, let relationships flow from your placement in the Father's house. Like children who naturally reflect their parents' mannerisms, placed sons express family characteristics. The Mirror Bible illuminates this in 2 Corinthians 3:18: "We are being transformed into his image with ever-increasing glory."

Chapter Summary

Huiothesia—placement as mature sons—isn't about becoming something we're not but about being positioned to express who we truly are. This placement transforms how we live, work, relate, and exercise authority. As placed sons, we naturally express divine life not through effort but through alignment with our true position in Christ. Like a monarch who must learn to operate from royal identity rather than earn it, we're discovering how to live from our position as mature sons and daughters. This placement isn't merely legal status but actual positioning in the family business of creation—we're not just given a title but equipped with everything necessary to represent family interests. Understanding this transforms every aspect of life: we approach challenges not as servants seeking approval but as sons authorized to manifest solutions; we engage in relationships not from need but from fullness; we exercise authority not through striving but through conscious alignment with our divine placement.

Reflection Questions

1. How might your daily life change if you consistently lived from placement rather than toward it?

2. What areas of your life still operate from effort rather than natural expression of divine life?

3. How could your exercise of authority transform if it flowed from placement rather than striving?

4. What practical steps can you take to maintain awareness of your position as a placed son?

5. How might your relationships change if you consistently lived from family placement?

Chapter 9
Nothing Can Separate

Unbreakable Union

In quantum physics, there exists a phenomenon called quantum entanglement where two particles become so deeply connected that what happens to one instantly affects the other, regardless of the distance between them. Even if these particles were on opposite ends of the universe, their connection would remain unbreakable. This natural phenomenon offers us a glimpse into a far more profound reality—our unbreakable union with God. The Mirror Bible expresses this eternal reality in Romans 8:38-39: "For I am convinced that neither death nor life, neither angels nor demons, neither the present nor the future, nor any powers... will be able to separate us from the love of God that is in Christ Jesus our Lord."

Consider how different this is from religious thinking that sees our relationship with God as fragile and dependent on our performance. The Passion Translation illuminates this distinction in Romans 8:15: "And you did not receive the 'spirit of religious duty,' leading you back into the fear of never being good enough. But you have received the 'Spirit of full acceptance,' enfolding you into the family of God."

Think about how a mother's DNA exists in every cell of her child's body. It's not a connection that can be broken—it's part of the very structure of who they are. Similarly, our union with God isn't something external that can be damaged or lost—it's woven into the very fabric of our being. The early church father Athanasius expressed this when he wrote, "The Son of God became man so that men might become sons of God."

Understanding Unbreakable Union

In the depths of the ocean exists one of nature's most remarkable phenomena—the Portuguese Man-of-War. What appears to be a single organism is actually a colony of thousands of individual organisms so perfectly united that they function as one being. While this natural wonder offers a glimpse of union, our union with God goes infinitely deeper. The Mirror Bible expresses this profound reality in 1 Corinthians 6:17: "The one being joined to the Lord exists as one spirit with him!"

Consider how a vine and its branches share one life system. Jesus used this very image, and The Passion Translation captures it beautifully in John 15:5: "I am the sprouting vine and you're my branches. As you live in union with me as your source, fruitfulness will stream from within you." This isn't just poetic language—it's describing an actual spiritual reality where His life and our life become one life.

Let me share a story that illuminates this truth. A master jeweler was teaching his apprentice about working with gold alloys. The apprentice asked if there was a way to separate the metals once they were properly alloyed. The master replied, "That's the beauty of a true alloy—the metals don't just mix, they form an entirely new substance. You can't separate them without destroying what they've become together." This perfectly illustrates our union with Christ—it's not a mixing of two separate lives but the formation of one new life.

The early church father Gregory of Nyssa described this union using the metaphor of iron in fire. When iron is placed in fire, it becomes so permeated with the fire's properties that you can't tell where the iron ends and the fire begins. Yet the iron remains iron, and the fire remains fire. The Mirror Bible illuminates this mystery in Galatians 2:20: "I am crucified with Christ: nevertheless I live; yet not I, but Christ lives in me."

Think about how light behaves when it passes through a prism. The light and the prism remain distinct, yet they create something neither could produce alone. The Passion Translation captures this dynamic in 2 Corinthians 3:18: "We can all draw close to him with the veil removed from our faces. And with no veil we all become like mirrors who brightly reflect the glory of the Lord Jesus."

This union transforms everything about how we understand our relationship with God:

Identity Fusion: Like a successful organ transplant where the body accepts the new organ as its own, our identity becomes so fused with Christ's that His life becomes our life. The Mirror Bible expresses this in Colossians 3:3-4: "Your life is now hidden with Christ in God. Christ is your life!"

Shared Consciousness: Similar to how quantum entangled particles share the same state, we share Christ's own consciousness. The Passion Translation renders 1 Corinthians 2:16: "But we possess the mind of Christ!"

Nature Participation: Just as grafted branches share the life of the tree, we participate in divine nature itself. The Mirror Bible illuminates this in 2 Peter 1:4: "He has given us his precious and magnificent promises... so that through them you may become partakers of the divine nature."

Beyond Performance to Position

Consider how gravity works. Objects don't have to perform or qualify to be affected by gravity—they simply exist within its field. Their position in the gravitational field, not their performance, determines their relationship to gravity. Similarly, our union with God isn't maintained by our performance but by our position in Christ. The Mirror Bible expresses this reality in Ephesians 2:6: "And He raised us up together with Him and seated us together in the heavenly realms in Christ Jesus."

Let me share a story that illuminates this truth. A renowned ballet company had two principal dancers. One constantly worried about her position, practicing obsessively and measuring herself against others. The other danced with complete freedom, knowing her position was secure. During a crucial performance, the first dancer, despite her perfect technique, appeared rigid and constrained. The second, though technically no better, danced with such freedom that she took the audience's breath away. The director later explained, "The difference wasn't in their ability but in their consciousness. One was trying to earn her position; the other was dancing from it."

The early church father Maximus the Confessor described this as moving from "motion toward God" to "motion in God." Like a planet that doesn't have to strive to stay in orbit—it simply moves within the gravitational field that holds it—we don't maintain union through effort but through resting in our position. The Passion Translation captures this in Colossians 2:6-7: "In the same way you received Jesus our Lord and Messiah by faith, continue your journey of faith, progressing further into your union with him!"

Think about how blood cells function in the body. They don't strive to belong to the body or work to maintain their connection—they simply function from their position within the circulatory system. The Mirror Bible illuminates this organic reality in John 15:4: "Remain in me, as I also remain in you. No branch can bear fruit by itself; it must remain in the vine."

This shift from performance to position transforms everything:

From Earning to Receiving: Like a child who naturally receives family DNA rather than earning it, we live from given life rather than achieved life. The Mirror Bible expresses this in 1 Corinthians 4:7: "What do you have that you did not receive?"
From Trying to Trusting: Similar to how a leaf doesn't try to photosynthesize—it simply receives sunlight from its position—we learn to trust our position rather than our effort. The Passion Translation renders Hebrews 4:3: "We who believe enter into that rest."

From Doing to Being: Just as a fish doesn't work at being a fish—it simply lives from its nature—we learn to live from who we are rather than trying to become. The Mirror Bible captures this in 2 Peter 1:4: "Through these he has given us his very great and precious promises, so that through them you may participate in the divine nature."

From Achievement to Alignment: Like a radio that doesn't create the music but aligns with the broadcast frequency, we learn to align with what's already true rather than trying to make something true. The Passion Translation illuminates this in 2 Corinthians 3:18: "We can all draw close to him with the veil removed from our faces."

Divine Love's Perfect Work

Consider how God's love deals with our false self. When Jesus said 'Two will be grinding at the mill; one will be taken and one will be left' (Matthew 24:41), He wasn't speaking of random selection but of divine separation—separating the false self from the true. When He declares to some, 'I never knew you' (Matthew 7:23), He's speaking to the false self, the constructed identity that was never real in the first place. The Mirror Bible expresses this reality in 2 Corinthians 5:17: 'Therefore if anyone is in Christ, the old creation has passed away. Behold, the fresh and new has come!'

This truth finds its ultimate expression in Revelation's imagery. In the end, only the Book of Life remains—the record of our true identity in Christ. All other books recording human works, achievements, and false identities are cast into the lake of fire. The Passion Translation illuminates this in Revelation 20:15: 'And anyone whose name was not found recorded in the Book of Life was thrown into the lake of fire.' This isn't about people being destroyed but about false identities being consumed, leaving only what's real—our true life hidden with Christ in God.

God's love is passionate about our true identity. Like a master sculptor removing everything that's not part of the masterpiece, divine love removes all that's not truly us until only Christ in us remains."

Love That Never Fails

In the world of nuclear physics, there exists a force called the "strong nuclear force"—the most powerful force in nature, holding atomic nuclei together against all other forces that would tear them apart. Yet this force pales in comparison to the love that holds us in union with God. The Mirror Bible expresses this unbreakable bond in Romans 8:38-39: "For I am persuaded beyond doubt that neither death nor life... nor any other created thing, shall be able to separate us from the love of God which is in Christ Jesus our Lord."

Consider how diamonds are formed. Under intense pressure and heat, carbon atoms form unbreakable bonds that create the hardest natural substance known to man. The Passion Translation captures this unbreakable nature of divine love in 1 Corinthians 13:8: "Love never fails. It never fades nor ends. Love never loses its value." This isn't poetic hyperbole—it's describing the actual nature of God's love.

Let me share a story that illuminates this truth. A master craftsman was known for creating unbreakable seals for royal documents. When asked his secret, he explained, "The strength isn't in the materials—it's in the bonding process. Under the right conditions, two substances don't just stick together; they become one new substance that can't be separated without destroying both." This perfectly illustrates how God's love doesn't just connect us to Him—it creates an unbreakable union.

The early church father John Chrysostom described God's love as "an ocean without shores or bottom." Like the gravitational field of a black hole that nothing can escape, divine love creates a field of attraction that nothing can break. The Mirror Bible illuminates this in Song of Solomon 8:6-7: "Love is as strong as death... Many waters cannot quench love, neither can floods drown it."

Think about how a mother's love for her child operates. The Passion Translation renders Isaiah 49:15-16: "Can a mother forget her nursing child? Can she feel no love for the child she has borne? But even if that were possible, I would not forget you! See, I have written your name on the palms of my hands." This isn't just emotional sentiment—it's revealing the unchangeable nature of divine love.

Key aspects of unfailing love:

Unconditional Nature: Like the sun that shines regardless of what's happening on Earth, God's love operates independent of conditions. The Mirror Bible expresses this in Romans 5:8: "But God demonstrates his own love for us in this: While we were still sinners, Christ died for us."

Undiminishable Strength: Similar to how gravity never weakens or tires, God's love never diminishes in power. The Passion Translation captures this in Jeremiah 31:3: "I have loved you with an everlasting love; therefore I have continued my faithfulness to you."

Unalterable Character: Just as light always behaves according to its nature, God's love consistently expresses His nature. The Mirror Bible illuminates this in 1 John 4:8: "God is love."

Living from Eternal Security

Consider how differently a tightrope walker performs with and without a safety harness. With the harness, they can attempt more daring moves, not because they're careless but because they're secure. Similarly, eternal security doesn't make us reckless—it makes us bold. The Mirror Bible expresses this reality in Hebrews 4:16: "Let us therefore come boldly to the throne of grace, that we may obtain mercy and find grace to help in time of need."

Let me share a story that illuminates this truth. A young pianist was preparing for her first major concert. Despite years of practice, she was paralyzed by fear of making mistakes. Her teacher shared a profound insight: "The audience didn't come to see if you can play perfectly—they came to hear the music. When you know your position on this stage is secure, you'll stop protecting yourself and start expressing the music." The next night, she played with such freedom that the audience was moved to tears. This perfectly illustrates how security in our position releases us to express divine life freely.

The early church father Irenaeus described this as "the freedom of glory." Like an eagle that soars effortlessly because it trusts the air currents, we can live freely because we trust our unbreakable union with God. The Passion Translation captures this in 2 Corinthians 3:17: "Now the Lord is the Spirit, and where the Spirit of the Lord is, there is freedom."

Think about how differently a child behaves in a secure home versus an insecure one. In a secure home, the child naturally explores, creates, and develops because they know their position is unshakeable. The Mirror Bible illuminates this in Romans 8:15: "The Spirit you received does not make you slaves, so that you live in fear again; rather, the Spirit you received brought about your adoption to sonship."

Practical expressions of living from security:

Face Challenges Boldly: Like a rock climber with a secure anchor, we can face any height because our position is secure. The Passion Translation renders Romans 8:37: "Yet in all these things we are more than conquerors through Him who loved us."

Express Life Freely: Similar to how a secure marriage produces natural expressions of love, security in God produces natural expressions of divine life. The Mirror Bible expresses this in Galatians 5:1: "It is for freedom that Christ has set us free."

Love Without Fear: Just as a secure parent can give unconditional love to their children, our security enables us to love without fear of rejection. The Passion Translation captures this in 1 John 4:18: "Perfect love drives out fear."

Create Without Anxiety: Like an artist who owns their studio and can experiment freely, security in our position releases creativity. The Mirror Bible illuminates this in Ephesians 2:10: "We are his poetry, created in Christ Jesus for good works."

Think about how the ocean's tides operate. They move with absolute freedom within the secure boundaries of gravitational forces. The early church fathers saw this as a picture of how security produces both freedom and faithfulness. The Mirror Bible expresses this paradox in 2 Corinthians 3:17-18: "Now the Lord is the Spirit, and where the Spirit of the Lord is, there is freedom. And we all, with unveiled face, beholding the glory of the Lord, are being transformed into the same image."

Manifesting Unbreakable Life

In the depths of ancient redwood forests, scientists have discovered something remarkable. When a mature redwood falls, new trees often sprout from its trunk, drawing life from the original root system. Even what appears to be death cannot stop the manifestation of life. This natural phenomenon illustrates how unbreakable life manifests—not through effort but through connection to an unbreakable source. The Mirror Bible expresses this reality in Colossians 3:3-4: "Your life is now hidden with Christ in God. Christ is your life!"

Consider how a master musician interprets a complex piece. They're not reading notes anymore—they're expressing music that's become part of their nature. The Passion Translation captures this natural expression in Galatians 2:20: "And now the essence of this new life is no longer mine, for the Anointed One lives his life through me—we live in union as one!"

Let me share a story that illuminates this truth. A master glassblower was teaching his apprentice about creating intricate designs. The apprentice was struggling, trying to force the glass into shape. The master said, "Stop trying to make the glass do what you want. Instead, become so aware of the glass's nature that you can let it express itself through you. When you and the glass move as one, the design emerges naturally." This perfectly illustrates how unbreakable life manifests—not through forcing but through flowing.

The early church father Gregory of Nyssa described this as "becoming by grace what God is by nature." Like a mirror that naturally reflects light when turned toward the sun, we naturally manifest divine life when aligned with our union. The Mirror Bible illuminates this in 2 Corinthians 3:18: "We are transfigured by the Spirit of the Lord in our constant beholding, from glory to glory."

Practical manifestations of unbreakable life:

Natural Expression: Like a river that doesn't strive to flow—it simply expresses its nature—divine life flows naturally through our union. The Passion Translation renders John 7:38: "Rivers of living water will flow from within them."

Effortless Impact: Similar to how light naturally dispels darkness without struggle, unbreakable life naturally affects our environment. The Mirror Bible expresses this in Matthew 5:14: "You are the light of the world."

Continuous Growth: Just as a healthy tree naturally produces fruit in season, divine life naturally manifests increasing expression. The Passion Translation captures this in John 15:5: "I am the vine;

you are the branches. If you remain in me and I in you, you will bear much fruit."

Resilient Response: Like a palm tree that bends in storms but doesn't break, unbreakable life manifests resilient strength. The Mirror Bible illuminates this in 2 Corinthians 4:8-9: "We are hard pressed on every side, but not crushed; perplexed, but not in despair."

Think about how the ocean maintains its essential nature regardless of surface conditions. Storms may create massive waves, but the depths remain undisturbed. Similarly, unbreakable life maintains its reality regardless of circumstances. The early church fathers called this "imperturbable peace"—not because life becomes easy, but because our union remains unshakeable.

Chapter Summary

Nothing can separate us from God's love because our union isn't maintained by our performance but by His nature. Like quantum entanglement at a spiritual level, we're inseparably united with divine life. This unbreakable union transforms how we live—not from fear of separation but from security of position. As we align with this reality, divine life naturally manifests through us, not as something we achieve but as something we express from our union. Just as a wave can never be separated from the ocean that forms it, our life is eternally bound up in divine life. This truth revolutionizes our entire approach to spirituality—we no longer strive to maintain connection with God but learn to live from the unbreakable union that already exists. Understanding this inseparable oneness frees us from performance-based living and releases us into natural expression of divine life through our unique personality and circumstances.

Reflection Questions

1. How might your daily life change if you lived consistently from the reality of unbreakable union?

2. What areas of your life still operate from fear of separation rather than security of position?

3. How could your relationships transform if you lived from unbreakable union rather than fear of rejection?

4. What practical steps can you take to maintain awareness of your inseparable union with God?

5. How might your response to challenges change if you lived from the reality that nothing can separate you from God's love?

Chapter 10

Working With God, Not For God

Partnership Over Performance

In the art of glass blowing, there comes a profound moment when master and apprentice achieve perfect synchronization. The apprentice's hands become so aligned with the master's movements that it's impossible to tell who's leading and who's following—they're simply moving as one. This artistic phenomenon illustrates the difference between working for God and working with God. The Mirror Bible expresses this reality in 1 Corinthians 3:9: "For we are God's co-workers, His fellow labourers."

Consider how different this is from religious service, where we work for God as if He's a distant employer rather than an indwelling presence. The Passion Translation illuminates this distinction in Galatians 4:7: "Now you are no longer a slave but God's own child. And since you are his child, God has made you his heir." We're not employees trying to please a boss—we're children expressing family nature.

Think about how a father and son might work together in a family business. The son isn't working to earn his place or prove his worth—he's working from his position as son, expressing and expanding the family legacy. The early church father Irenaeus captured this when he wrote, "The glory of God is man fully alive." This isn't about serving God through effort but about expressing God through union.

The Language of Union

Our very language often reveals a separation mindset. Consider how small prepositions can mask huge theological truths: we say 'faith in Christ' when scripture speaks of living by 'the faith of Christ.' The Mirror Bible expresses this in Galatians 2:20: 'The life I now live, I live by the faith of the Son of God.' It's not our faith reaching toward Him but His faith expressing through us.

Similarly, we often speak of 'working with God' as if we're two separate parties cooperating, when in reality, it's Christ's own life working through us. The Passion Translation captures this in Philippians 2:13: 'God himself is at work in you, inspiring you to want those things which please him and to work for them.'

Many believers still talk about 'inviting God's presence' when He already dwells within us. Through Christ's vicarious humanity—His living, dying, and rising as us—everything has become an 'inside job.' The Mirror Bible illuminates this in Colossians 1:27: 'Christ in you, the hope of glory!'

From Service to Partnership

In traditional Japanese arts, there exists a profound concept called "isshin-denshin"—a state where master and student achieve such perfect communion that thoughts transfer without words. What begins as a master-servant relationship evolves into something far deeper—a partnership of shared consciousness. The Mirror Bible expresses this evolution in John 15:15: "I no longer call you servants, because a servant does not know his master's business. Instead, I have called you friends, for everything that I learned from my Father I have made known to you."

Consider how different this is from religious service. When working for God, we're constantly trying to discern His will as if it's something external to us. But The Passion Translation illuminates a different reality in Philippians 2:13: "God himself is at work in you, inspiring you to want those things which please him and to work for them." We're not guessing at God's will—we're expressing it from within.

Let me share a story that captures this truth. A renowned dance company had two principal dancers. The first approached each performance trying to perfectly execute the choreographer's vision, resulting in technically flawless but somehow lifeless performances. The second had learned to so deeply internalize the choreographer's heart that she could improvise while remaining perfectly true to his vision. The director explained, "The first dancer works for the choreography; the second works with it. The first serves the dance; the second expresses it."

The early church father Maximus the Confessor described this as "natural movement according to nature." Like a bird that doesn't need instructions to fly—it simply expresses its nature—we learn to express divine life naturally rather than following external rules. The Mirror Bible captures this in Galatians 5:25: "If we live by the Spirit, let us also walk by the Spirit."

Think about how a master violinist and accompanist work together. At the highest level, they're not following each other—they're expressing one musical consciousness. The Passion Translation renders 1 Corinthians 6:17: "But the one who joins himself to the Lord is mingled into one spirit with him."

This shift from service to partnership manifests in several ways:

From External Direction to Internal Flow: Like a river that doesn't need directions to flow downstream—it simply follows its nature—we learn to move with divine life rather than following rules. The Mirror Bible expresses this in Romans 8:14: "For all who are led by the Spirit of God are sons of God."

From Duty to Delight: Similar to how young lovers don't serve each other from obligation but from joy, partnership with God flows from delight rather than duty. The Passion Translation captures this in Psalm 40:8: "I delight to do Your will, O my God; Your law is within my heart."

From Distance to Union: Just as quantum entangled particles operate as one regardless of distance, we work with God from union rather than across a gap. The Mirror Bible illuminates this in Colossians 1:27: "Christ in you, the hope of glory."

Divine Collaboration

In the world of improvisational jazz, there exists a phenomenon musicians call "being in the pocket"—a state where individual musicians become so attuned to each other that the music seems to play itself through them. This natural wonder illustrates true divine collaboration. The Mirror Bible expresses this reality in 2 Corinthians 6:1: "As God's co-workers we urge you not to receive God's grace in vain."

Consider how different this is from the religious model where we work hard and then ask God to bless our efforts. The Passion Translation illuminates true collaboration in John 5:17,19: "My Father is always working, and so am I... the Son can do nothing by himself. He does only what he sees the Father doing. Whatever the Father does, the Son also does." This isn't about independent action but synchronized expression.

Let me share a story that captures this truth. A master potter was teaching his apprentice about centering clay on the wheel. The apprentice kept trying to force the clay into position. The master placed his hands over the apprentice's and said, "Stop trying to center the clay. Let me center your hands, and the clay will center itself." After experiencing this guided movement, the apprentice exclaimed, "I wasn't working with the clay at all—I was fighting it! Now I understand: my hands aren't centering the clay; they're participating in its centering."

The early church father Gregory of Nyssa described this as "synergy with God." Like a sail that doesn't create wind but aligns with it, we learn to align with divine movement rather than generating our own. The Mirror Bible captures this in Philippians

2:13: "God is working in you, giving you the desire and the power to do what pleases him."

Think about how a mother and child naturally coordinate their movements when walking together. There's no conscious effort to match steps—they naturally synchronize. The Passion Translation renders Acts 17:28: "For in him we live and move and have our being."

Key aspects of divine collaboration:

Synchronized Movement: Like figure skaters who move as one, true collaboration means moving in perfect harmony with divine life. The Mirror Bible expresses this in Galatians 2:20: "I no longer live, but Christ lives in me."

Shared Consciousness: Similar to how a highly trained surgical team anticipates each other's needs without words, we learn to move with divine intention naturally. The Passion Translation illuminates this in 1 Corinthians 2:16: "But we possess the mind of Christ!"

Natural Flow: Just as water naturally follows the path of least resistance, divine collaboration flows without strain or effort. The Mirror Bible captures this in Matthew 11:30: "For my yoke is easy and my burden is light."

Natural Co-Creation

In quantum mechanics, there's a remarkable phenomenon called quantum superposition where particles exist in multiple states simultaneously until they're observed. Similarly, when we're aligned with divine life, possibilities we couldn't imagine on our own naturally emerge through our collaboration. The Mirror Bible expresses this creative reality in Ephesians 2:10: "We are his poetry, we are the words of his story, created in Christ Jesus to give expression to his intent."

Consider how a vine expresses its life through branches. The branches don't strain to produce fruit—they simply allow the vine's life to flow through them. The Passion Translation illuminates this natural creativity in John 15:5: "I am the sprouting vine and you're my branches. As you live in union with me as your source, fruitfulness will stream from within you."

Let me share a story that captures this truth. A renowned composer was asked about his creative process. He replied, "I don't create the music—I discover it. It's as if the music already exists in another dimension, and my role is to let it flow into this one. The less I try to control it, the more magnificent it becomes." This perfectly illustrates natural co-creation—not generating something new but participating in what God is already doing.

The early church father Maximus the Confessor described this as "becoming by grace what God is by nature." Like a prism that doesn't create light but reveals its hidden colours, we don't generate creativity—we manifest divine creativity through our unique design. The Mirror Bible captures this in 2 Corinthians 4:7: "We have this treasure in earthen vessels, that the excellency of the power may be of God, and not of us."

Think about how DNA works. Every cell contains the complete pattern for the whole body, yet each cell expresses that pattern uniquely according to its position and purpose. The Passion Translation renders 1 Corinthians 12:4-6: "There are different kinds of spiritual gifts, but the same Spirit is the source of them all... God works in different ways, but it is the same God who does the work in all of us."

Essential aspects of natural co-creation:

Alignment Before Action: Like a satellite dish that must be properly aligned to receive signals, we learn to align with divine creativity before attempting to create. The Mirror Bible expresses this in John 5:19: "The Son can do nothing of Himself, but what He sees the Father do."

Flow vs. Force: Similar to how a skilled surfer moves with the wave rather than fighting it, we learn to move with divine creative flow. The Passion Translation captures this in Acts 17:28: "In him we live and move and have our being."

Unique Expression: Just as every snowflake manifests the same principles of crystallization uniquely, each of us expresses divine creativity in our own way. The Mirror Bible illuminates this in 1 Corinthians 12:11: "All these are empowered by one and the same Spirit, who apportions to each one individually as he wills."

Family Business Model

In traditional Italian artisan families, craft secrets are passed down not as mere techniques but as living heritage. A young apprentice doesn't just learn skills from their father—they absorb a way of being, a family consciousness about the craft. The Mirror Bible expresses this family dynamic in Romans 8:17: "And if we are children, then we are heirs—heirs of God and co-heirs with Christ."

Consider how different this is from the employer-employee model where work is based on contract rather than covenant. The Passion Translation illuminates this distinction in Galatians 4:7: "Now you are no longer a slave but God's own child. And since you are his child, God has made you his heir." In a family business, work isn't about earning—it's about expressing and expanding family legacy.

Let me share a story that captures this truth. A master watchmaker was teaching his son the family craft. The son was frustrated, trying to memorize every technical detail. The father said, "Stop trying to remember and start trying to understand. These aren't just techniques—they're our family's way of seeing time itself. When you grasp that, the details will flow naturally." This perfectly illustrates how family business operates from shared consciousness rather than mere instruction.

The early church father Irenaeus described this as "participating in the Father's business." Like a son who naturally picks up his father's business instincts through close association, we learn to operate in divine business through intimate relationship. The Mirror Bible captures this in Luke 2:49: "Did you not know that I must be about my Father's business?"

Think about how DNA carries not just physical traits but behavioral tendencies. Children often naturally mirror their parents' way of thinking and working without conscious effort. The Passion Translation renders 2 Peter 1:4: "Through these he has given us his very great and precious promises, so that through them you may participate in the divine nature."

Key aspects of the family business model:

Inherited Authority: Like a son who naturally carries family authority, our authority comes from relationship rather than position. The Mirror Bible expresses this in Luke 10:19: "Behold, I give unto you power... over all the power of the enemy."

Shared Resources: Similar to how family resources are naturally available to family members, we have access to all divine resources. The Passion Translation illuminates this in Philippians 4:19: "And my God will supply all your needs according to His riches in glory in Christ Jesus."

Natural Expansion: Just as a healthy family business naturally grows and develops, divine business expands through relationship rather than effort. The Mirror Bible captures this in Mark 4:26-28: "The kingdom of God is like a man who scatters seed on the ground... All by itself the soil produces grain."

Living from Union

In the world of quantum physics, there's a state called "quantum coherence" where particles become so perfectly aligned that they operate as a single system. Individual particles maintain their distinct identity while functioning in perfect unity. This natural phenomenon illustrates how we're meant to live and work with God. The Mirror Bible expresses this reality in 1 Corinthians 6:17: "The one being joined to the Lord exists as one spirit with him!"

Consider how a master ballet dancer moves. At the highest level, they're not following choreography—they're expressing music through their very being. The Passion Translation illuminates this natural expression in Galatians 2:20: "And now the essence of this new life is no longer mine, for the Anointed One lives his life through me—we live in union as one!"

Let me share a story that captures this truth. A master calligrapher was asked about achieving perfect brushstrokes. He replied, "The secret isn't in the hand but in the heart. When your heart is in perfect harmony with the character you're writing, your hand simply follows. The stroke isn't something you do—it's something you participate in." This perfectly illustrates living from union—not trying to live for God but letting His life express through us.

The early church father Maximus the Confessor described this as "natural movement according to nature." Like a river that doesn't strive to flow— it simply expresses its nature—we learn to let divine life flow naturally through our union. The Mirror Bible captures this in John 15:4-5: "Remain in me, as I also remain in you... for apart from me you can do nothing."

Practical expressions of living from union:

Begin Each Day from Union: Like a musician tuning their instrument before playing, start each day by aligning with your union with God. The Passion Translation renders Colossians 3:3: "Your secret life is now hidden in God as you are placed into the revelation of the life of Christ."

Face Challenges from Unity: Instead of tackling problems alone and asking for help, operate from the reality that His life and yours are one. The Mirror Bible expresses this in 1 Corinthians 1:30: "It is because of him that you are in Christ Jesus."

Work from Rest: Similar to how a master artist works with seemingly effortless flow, let work emerge from your rest in union rather than striving. The Mirror Bible illuminates this in Hebrews 4:3: "We who have believed enter that rest."

Build Relationships from Oneness: Just as branches naturally share the vine's life with other branches, let relationships flow from your union with divine life. The Passion Translation captures this in 1 John 4:19: "We love because he first loved us."

Think about how light travels through space. It doesn't effort its way forward—it simply expresses its nature. Living from union isn't about trying harder but about expressing what's already true. The early church fathers called this "natural living"—when divine life becomes so natural it flows without conscious effort.

Chapter Summary

Working with God rather than for God transforms everything about how we live and serve. Like a family business where children naturally express and expand family legacy, we're called to work from union rather than duty. This isn't about trying to achieve something new but about manifesting what's already true—our inseparable union with divine life. As partners rather than servants, we discover a new way of operating that flows from relationship rather than obligation. Just as a son naturally carries forward the family vision because it's part of his identity, we find ourselves expressing divine purpose not through external pressure but through internal alignment. This shift from working for God to working with Him revolutionizes our approach to every task and challenge—we move from striving to please Him to naturally expressing His life and purpose through our unique gifts and calling.

Reflection Questions

1. How might your daily work change if you approached it from union rather than duty?

2. What areas of your life still operate from an employer-employee mindset with God?

3. How could your creativity flow differently if you saw it as participating in divine creativity?

4. What practical steps can you take to maintain awareness of working with God rather than for Him?

5. How might your relationships transform if you lived consistently from union rather than separation?

Chapter 11

Displacing Modern Giants

Overcoming Present-Day Strongholds

When Israel first spied out the Promised Land, they saw giants and called themselves grasshoppers in comparison. Forty years later, facing the same giants, they saw themselves as sons and called the giants bread for their eating. What changed wasn't the size of the giants—what changed was their consciousness of who they were. The Mirror Bible expresses this transformation in Numbers 14:9: "Do not fear the people of the land, for they are bread for us. Their protection has been removed from them, and the Lord is with us!"

Today's giants may not be physical Nephilim, but they're just as real: the giant of separation consciousness that makes us feel distant from God, the giant of performance-based acceptance that keeps us striving, the giant of religious duty that obscures grace, the giant of orphan thinking that blinds us to our true identity. The Passion Translation illuminates our victory over these giants in 1 John 4:4: "Little children, you can be certain that you belong to God and have conquered them, for the One who is living in you is far greater than the one who is in the world."

Think about how differently David approached Goliath compared to Israel's army. Where they saw a giant too big to fight, he saw a target too big to miss. The early church father Athanasius captured this perspective when he wrote, "What seems impossible to men is possible to God, and what appears as weakness to the world manifests as strength through faith."

Modern Giants Identified

In ancient warfare, giants relied on intimidation as much as strength. Similarly, today's giants use deception and intimidation to prevent us from possessing our inheritance. The Mirror Bible expresses this reality in 2 Corinthians 10:4-5: "The weapons of our warfare are not carnal but mighty through God for pulling down strongholds, casting down arguments and every high thing that exalts itself against the knowledge of God."

Let me share a story that illuminates this truth. A master jeweler was training his apprentice to identify genuine gems. The apprentice was frustrated by how convincing some fakes appeared. The master explained, "The counterfeits aren't trying to be different from real gems—they're trying to look exactly like them. That's why knowing the authentic intimately is more important than studying fakes." This perfectly illustrates how modern giants operate—not by being obviously false, but by subtly distorting truth.

The primary giants we face today include:

The Giant of Separation Consciousness: Like the serpent in Eden suggesting God was withholding something, this giant wants us to believe we're separated from God's love and life. The Passion Translation captures our true reality in Romans 8:39: "There is nothing in our present or future circumstances that can weaken his love toward us."

The Giant of Performance-Based Acceptance: This giant wants us to believe we must earn what God has freely given. The Mirror Bible expresses our true position in Ephesians 1:6: "The same love he has for his Beloved Son is his love for you! We are highly favoured in him!"

The Giant of Religious Works: This massive deception tries to replace grace with human effort, making us slaves to religious performance. The Mirror Bible illuminates truth in Galatians 5:1: "Christ has set us free to live a free life. So take your stand! Never again let anyone put a harness of slavery on you."

The Giant of False Identity: Like a skilled identity thief, this giant works to keep us from knowing who we really are—sons of God ranking higher than angels. The Passion Translation renders 1 John 3:1: "Look with wonder at the depth of the Father's marvellous love that he has lavished on us! He has called us and made us his very own children!"

The Giant of Condemnation: This giant wants to keep us focused on our sins rather than Christ's finished work. The Mirror Bible expresses our true state in Romans 8:1: "There is now no condemnation for those who are in Christ Jesus."

Think about how viruses work. They don't attack the body directly—they insert their own code into cells, making them malfunction. Similarly, these giants don't typically confront us directly—they insert false beliefs that distort our understanding of:

Who God Really Is: They don't want us to know God as infinitely loving, gracious, merciful, and forgiving. The Passion Translation illuminates His nature in 1 John 4:16: "God is love, and all who live in love live in God, and God lives in them."

Who We Really Are: They work tirelessly to hide our true identity as sons of God. The Mirror Bible captures our reality in Romans 8:14: "For all who are led by the Spirit of God are sons of God."

What We Really Have: Like squatters trying to prevent rightful owners from claiming property, these giants want to hide that God has given us all things in Christ. The Mirror Bible expresses our inheritance in Ephesians 1:3: "Blessed be the God and Father of our Lord Jesus Christ, who has blessed us with every spiritual blessing in the heavenly places in Christ."

The Seven Mindset Giants

Just as Israel faced seven specific nations in Canaan, we face seven corresponding mindset giants today. The Mirror Bible expresses our authority over these in Deuteronomy 7:1-2: "When the LORD your God brings you into the land you are entering to possess and drives out before you many nations... you must defeat them totally."

The Hittites (Terror): This mindset giant produces fear-based living, making us react from anxiety rather than respond from sonship. The Passion Translation captures our victory over fear in 2 Timothy 1:7: "For God has not given us a spirit of fear, but of power and of love and of a sound mind."

The Girgashites (Earthly Mindedness): This giant keeps us focused on natural limitations rather than supernatural possibilities. The Mirror Bible expresses our true perspective in Colossians 3:1-2: "Since you have been raised up with Christ, keep seeking the things above, where Christ is."

The Amorites (Pride/Self-Exaltation): This mindset elevates self-achievement over grace, making us rely on our strength rather than God's life. The Mirror Bible illuminates truth in James 4:6: "God opposes the proud but gives grace to the humble."

The Canaanites (Unstable/Wavering): This giant produces double-mindedness, making us unstable in our identity and inheritance. The Passion Translation renders James 1:6-8: "When you ask him, be sure that your faith is in God alone. Do not waver..."

The Perizzites (Separation): This mindset creates artificial barriers between us and God, between sacred and secular. The Mirror Bible expresses our unity in 1 Corinthians 6:17: "The one being joined to the Lord exists as one spirit with him!"

The Hivites (Worldly Compromise): This giant subtly leads us to compromise our true identity for worldly acceptance. The Passion

Translation captures our distinction in Romans 12:2: "Stop imitating the ideals and opinions of the culture around you."

The Jebusites (Religious Performance): This mindset turns relationship into religion, replacing grace with works. The Mirror Bible illuminates freedom in Galatians 5:1: "Christ has set us free to live a free life. So take your stand! Never again let anyone put a harness of slavery on you."

These ancient enemies represent modern mindset strongholds that must be displaced by truth. Just as Israel possessed the land by displacing these nations, we possess our inheritance by displacing these false mindsets with true identity consciousness.

From Fear to Faith

Consider how a master martial artist handles a larger opponent. Instead of reacting with fear to the opponent's size, they see that very size as leverage they can use. The Mirror Bible expresses this perspective shift in Numbers 14:9: "Do not fear the people of the land, for they are bread for us." What appears as a threat to fear consciousness becomes nourishment to faith consciousness.

Let me share a story that illuminates this truth. A seasoned mountain guide was training new climbers about facing steep cliffs. One trainee was paralyzed by the height. The guide said, "Stop looking down at the drop and start looking up at your anchor. The size of the cliff doesn't determine your safety—your connection to the anchor does." This perfectly illustrates how we overcome giants—not by denying their size but by focusing on our greater reality in Christ.

The early church father Athanasius described this as "seeing with resurrection eyes." Like someone who knows the end of the story while watching its beginning, we face giants from the perspective of already-accomplished victory. The Passion Translation captures this in 1 John 5:4: "For every child of God defeats this evil world, and we achieve this victory through our faith."

Think about how different David's approach to Goliath was. While others focused on Goliath's size compared to themselves, David focused on Goliath's size compared to God. The Mirror Bible illuminates this perspective in 1 Samuel 17:47: "The battle is the Lord's."

Key aspects of moving from fear to faith:

Perspective Shift: Instead of seeing giants as obstacles to overcome, we see them as opportunities to demonstrate sonship. The Mirror Bible expresses this in Romans 8:37: "In all these things we are super conquerors through him who loved us!"

Identity Awareness: Like a lion who doesn't need to be taught to roar, we learn to live from who we are rather than fight for who we want to become. The Passion Translation renders 1 John 4:17: "As he is, so are we in this world!"

Rest-Based Engagement: Similar to how a skilled surfer faces huge waves from a position of rest rather than reaction, we face giants from our rest in Christ. The Mirror Bible captures this in Hebrews 4:3: "We who have believed enter that rest."

Position Over Performance

In the game of chess, a piece's power doesn't come from its individual efforts but from its position on the board. A pawn in the right position can be more decisive than a queen in the wrong one. Similarly, victory over giants comes from our position in Christ, not our performance against them. The Mirror Bible expresses this reality in Ephesians 2:6: "And He raised us up together with Him and seated us together in the heavenly realms in Christ Jesus."

Consider how gravity works. Objects don't overcome gravity's pull through effort—they overcome it through position. A plane doesn't fight gravity; it uses principles of lift that work regardless of gravity's strength. The Passion Translation captures this positional truth in Colossians 3:1: "Since you have been raised to new life with Christ, set your sights on the realities of heaven, where Christ sits in the place of honour at God's right hand."

Let me share a story that illuminates this truth. A master conductor was asked why some musicians strain to play while others seem effortless. He explained, "The struggling ones are trying to create music through effort. The effortless ones have found their position in the music—they're not creating it, they're participating in what's already there." This perfectly illustrates how position trumps performance in overcoming giants.

The early church father Gregory of Nyssa described this as "movement according to nature." Like a river that flows effortlessly because of its position relative to sea level, we overcome not through striving but through resting in our position in Christ. The Mirror Bible illuminates this in Romans 8:37: "In all these things we are super conquerors through him who loved us!"

Think about how an electrical circuit works. Current flows not because individual electrons try harder, but because they're properly positioned in relation to the power source. The Passion Translation renders Philippians 4:13: "I find the strength to face all conditions by the power that Christ gives me."

Key aspects of position over performance:

Authority from Location: Like an ambassador whose authority comes from their position representing their nation, our authority over giants comes from our position in Christ. The Mirror Bible expresses this in Luke 10:19: "Behold, I give unto you power... over all the power of the enemy."

Rest-Based Victory: Similar to how a skilled martial artist uses their opponent's strength against them through proper positioning, we overcome through resting in our position rather than striving in our performance. The Passion Translation captures this in Matthew 11:28-30: "Come to me... and you will find rest for your souls."

Natural Expression: Just as a fruit tree naturally produces fruit because of its connection to the root system, victory flows naturally from our position rather than our effort. The Mirror Bible illuminates this in John 15:5: "I am the vine, you are the branches. He who abides in Me, and I in him, bears much fruit."

Displacement Through Rest

In physics, there's a principle called "displacement" where an object immersed in fluid displaces its own volume of that fluid. It doesn't fight to push the fluid out—its mere presence causes natural displacement. This illustrates how rest in our true identity naturally displaces giants. The Mirror Bible expresses this reality in Hebrews 4:3: "We who have believed enter that rest."

Consider how light works. Darkness isn't overcome through fighting it—light's mere presence naturally displaces darkness. The Passion Translation captures this natural displacement in John 1:5: "The light shines in the darkness, and the darkness has not overcome it." True rest in our identity naturally displaces false mindsets.

Let me share a story that illuminates this truth. A master sculptor was teaching his student about creating space in design. The student was laboriously trying to carve empty spaces into the stone. The master said, "Stop trying to create emptiness. Instead, place solid forms precisely, and space naturally appears around them. The presence of substance creates space—you don't have to fight for it." This perfectly illustrates how resting in truth naturally displaces lies.

The early church father Maximus the Confessor described this as "effortless effort." Like how a healthy body naturally fights infection not through conscious striving but through its mere presence of health, truth displaces lies through its mere presence. The Mirror Bible illuminates this in John 8:32: "And you will know the truth, and the truth will set you free."

Think about how oil and water interact. When oil is poured into water, it naturally rises to the top—not through effort but through its nature. The Passion Translation renders 2 Corinthians 3:17: "Now the Lord is the Spirit, and where the Spirit of the Lord is, there is freedom."

Displacing these giants ultimately comes down to whose voice we believe—God's or others' (including our own). The Mirror Bible expresses this battle in 2 Corinthians 10:4-5: 'We are demolishing arguments and every high-minded thing that exalts itself against the knowledge of God. We are taking every thought captive to the obedience of Christ.'

Consider how this played out in biblical encounters:
- When Gideon saw himself as the least in his father's house, God called him a mighty warrior
- When Zacchaeus was defined by his profession and reputation, Jesus called him a son of Abraham
- When the woman at the well was defined by her past, Jesus saw her as an evangelist

As Amos 3:3 asks, 'Can two walk together unless they are agreed?' The displacement of giants happens when we begin agreeing with God's perspective rather than:
- What others say about us
- What we say about ourselves
- What our performance suggests
- What our past dictates
- What our circumstances indicate

The Mirror Bible captures this transformative agreement in 2 Corinthians 5:16: 'From now on we regard no one according to the flesh.' When we agree with God's perspective, giants that once seemed insurmountable become bread for our eating.

Key aspects of displacement through rest:

Natural Authority: Like how a higher pressure system naturally displaces a lower one, higher truth naturally displaces lower mindsets. The Mirror Bible expresses this in 2 Corinthians 10:5: "We demolish arguments and every pretension that sets itself up against the knowledge of God."

Present Reality: Similar to how a solid object's presence naturally displaces air, our present reality in Christ naturally displaces false identities. The Passion Translation captures this in Colossians 3:3: "Your secret life is now hidden in God."

Effortless Impact: Just as heat naturally displaces cold through its mere presence, truth naturally impacts environments through its being rather than its doing. The Mirror Bible illuminates this in Matthew 5:14: "You are the light of the world."

Living Above Giants

In the world of aviation, there's a phenomenon called "getting above the weather." While storms rage below, planes can fly in perfect calm above the clouds. This illustrates how we're called to live—not fighting giants at their level but living from our position above them. The Mirror Bible expresses this reality in Ephesians 2:6: "He raised us up together and seated us together in the heavenly places in Christ Jesus."

Consider how an eagle responds to a storm. Instead of fighting the wind, it uses those very winds to soar higher. The Passion Translation captures this upward perspective in Isaiah 40:31: "But those who wait upon the Lord will renew their strength; they will mount up with wings like eagles."

Let me share a story that illuminates this truth. A master chess player was known for his unusual calm during matches. When asked his secret, he explained, "Most players are thinking three moves ahead on the board. I learned to think from above the board—seeing patterns from a higher perspective changes everything. What looks like a crisis at ground level becomes an opportunity from above." This perfectly illustrates living above giants rather than fighting them at their level.

The early church father Gregory of Nyssa described this as "participating in divine nature." Like a satellite that operates above Earth's turbulence, we're called to live from our position in Christ above life's giants. The Mirror Bible illuminates this in Colossians 3:1-2: "Since, then, you have been raised with Christ, set your hearts on things above, where Christ is, seated at the right hand of God."

Practical expressions of living above giants:

Begin Each Day from Position: Like a pilot who gets above the weather before setting course, start each day by aligning with your position in Christ. The Passion Translation renders Romans 6:11: "Consider yourselves dead to sin but alive to God in Christ Jesus."

See from Heaven's Perspective: Similar to how a mountaintop view transforms our understanding of the valley, let heavenly perspective interpret earthly circumstances. The Mirror Bible expresses this in 2 Corinthians 4:18: "We do not look at the things which are seen, but at the things which are not seen."

Operate from Rest: Just as a soaring bird rests in wind currents rather than fighting them, let rest be your operational base. The Passion Translation captures this in Matthew 11:28-30: "Come to me... and you will find rest for your souls."

Manifest Through Being: Like light that transforms darkness through its mere presence, let your true identity naturally impact environments. The Mirror Bible illuminates this in 1 John 4:17: "As he is, so are we in this world!"

Think about how the sun always shines above storm clouds. From Earth's perspective, storms can hide the sun, but from above, the sun never stops shining. Living above giants means maintaining heaven's perspective regardless of Earth's conditions.

Chapter Summary

Modern giants, whether the seven mindsets of the "-ites" or other false belief systems, are displaced not through fighting but through living from our true position in Christ. Like Israel possessing the Promised Land, we displace giants through rest in our inheritance rather than striving in our own strength. When we live from the consciousness of our union with Christ, these limiting mindsets naturally give way to the reality of who we are as sons and daughters. Our victory over these giants comes not from battle but from being—simply manifesting our true identity in Christ. Just as light naturally displaces darkness without struggle, our awareness of our inheritance naturally displaces false beliefs and limiting patterns. This transformative process mirrors how dawn naturally dispels night—not through conflict but through the simple presence of greater reality. As we grow in consciousness of our true identity and inheritance, these giants lose their power and influence, displaced by the effortless expression of who we really are in Christ.

Reflection Questions

1. How might your approach to challenges change if you lived from position rather than performance?

2. What areas of your life still operate at the giants' level rather than above them?

3. How could your impact increase if you focused on presence rather than performance?

4. What practical steps can you take to maintain heaven's perspective in daily life?

5. How might your rest become more effective than your previous fighting?

Chapter 12
Living from Union

One Spirit Reality

In quantum physics, there exists a state called "quantum coherence" where particles become so perfectly aligned that they function as a single system while maintaining their distinct identities. This natural phenomenon offers us a glimpse into a greater reality—our union with God. The Mirror Bible expresses this profound truth in 1 Corinthians 6:17: "The one being joined to the Lord exists as one spirit with him!"

Consider how different this is from religious approaches that treat unity with God as a distant goal to achieve. The Passion Translation illuminates our present reality in Colossians 3:3-4: "Your secret life is now hidden in God as you are placed into the revelation of the life of Christ. And when Christ who is your life is revealed, then you will also be revealed with him in glory!"

Think about how a master musician becomes one with their instrument. At the highest level, there's no separation between musician and music—they're so united that music flows effortlessly through their union. The early church father Gregory of Nyssa described this as "movement according to nature," where divine life flows naturally through our union rather than through effort.

Out Heart-Brain Coherence

Scientists have discovered a fascinating phenomenon called heart-brain coherence. When the heart and brain achieve synchronization, the entire body functions at optimal levels. Studies show that the heart actually sends more signals to the brain than vice versa, and when these signals are in harmony, it produces extraordinary results in both physical and mental performance. This natural wonder illustrates how union consciousness works.

The Mirror Bible expresses this coherence in Philippians 2:13: 'God is working in you, giving you the desire (heart) and the power (mind) to do what pleases him.' Just as the heart represents our true self and the brain our conscious thoughts and reasoning, living from union means bringing both into perfect alignment with Christ's life within us.

This isn't about the mind controlling the heart or the heart bypassing the mind—it's about Christ working in us, through us, and as us in perfect harmony. The Passion Translation captures this unity in 1 Corinthians 2:16: 'But we possess the mind of Christ!' Through His vicarious humanity, Christ aligns every aspect of our being—heart, mind, and body—into coherent expression of His life.

Like a perfectly tuned instrument where every string vibrates in harmony, our entire being resonates with divine life when we live from union rather than toward it.

Understanding One Spirit Reality

In the depths of oceans, there exists a remarkable phenomenon called bioluminescence, where tiny organisms become so united with light that they actually become light-producers themselves. What they contain, they become. This natural wonder illustrates our union with God—we're not just containing divine life; we're becoming expressions of it. The Mirror Bible captures this reality in 2 Peter 1:4: "Through these he has given us his very great and precious promises, so that through them you may participate in the divine nature."

Consider how a grafted branch works. It doesn't strive to receive life from the vine—it's so perfectly united that the vine's life becomes its life. The Passion Translation illuminates this in John 15:5: "I am the sprouting vine and you're my branches. As you live in union with me as your source, fruitfulness will stream from within you."

Let me share a story that captures this truth. A master glassblower was teaching his apprentice about creating complex pieces. The apprentice was struggling, trying to impose his will on the glass. The master said, "Stop trying to control the glass. Instead, become so one with its nature that your hands know what it wants to do before it does. True mastery isn't domination—it's union." This perfectly illustrates how one spirit reality works—not through control but through union.

The early church father Athanasius expressed this when he wrote, "God became man so that man might become divine." Like iron in fire that becomes so permeated with the fire's properties that you can't tell where iron ends and fire begins, we're called to live in such union that divine life naturally expresses through us. The Mirror Bible expresses this in Colossians 1:27: "Christ in you, the hope of glory!"

Think about how water molecules form clouds. Individual molecules don't strain to create cloud formations—they simply express their united nature. The Passion Translation renders 1 John 4:17: "As he is, so are we in this world!" This isn't poetic language—it's describing our actual spiritual reality.

Key aspects of one spirit reality:

Shared Consciousness: Like quantum entangled particles that instantly share the same state, we share Christ's own consciousness. The Mirror Bible illuminates this in 1 Corinthians 2:16: "We have the mind of Christ!"

United Identity: Similar to how light and its radiance can't be separated, our identity is inseparably united with Christ's. The Passion Translation captures this in Galatians 2:20: "And now the essence of this new life is no longer mine, for the Anointed One lives his life through me."

Natural Flow: Just as blood naturally flows through every part of the body, divine life naturally flows through our union. The Mirror Bible expresses this in John 7:38: "Rivers of living water will flow from within them."

Natural Expression of Union

In the art of traditional Japanese brush painting, there's a state called "*mushin*" where the artist becomes so one with the brush that the painting seems to create itself. This isn't about losing identity but about such perfect union that expression becomes effortless. The Mirror Bible captures this natural flow in Galatians 2:20: "I am crucified with Christ: nevertheless I live; yet not I, but Christ lives in me."

Consider how a mother naturally expresses maternal instincts. She doesn't consult a manual on how to love her child—love flows naturally from her union with maternal nature. The Passion Translation illuminates this natural expression in 1 John 4:19: "We love because he first loved us." Divine nature expresses itself as naturally through us as maternal nature expresses through a mother.

Let me share a story that captures this truth. A master violinist was teaching his student who was struggling to play a complex piece. The student was meticulously thinking through every note. The master said, "Stop trying to play the music and let the music play you. When you're truly one with it, your fingers will know what to do before your mind does." This perfectly illustrates how union expresses itself—not through effort but through alignment.

The early church father Maximus the Confessor described this as "natural movement according to nature." Like a river that doesn't strain to flow downstream—it simply expresses its nature—divine life flows naturally through our union. The Mirror Bible expresses this in Philippians 2:13: "God is working in you, giving you the desire and the power to do what pleases him."

Think about how a healthy immune system works. It doesn't need instructions to fight infection—it naturally expresses its protective nature. The Passion Translation renders 1 John 4:17: "As he is, so are we in this world!" Just as health naturally expresses through a healthy body, divine life naturally expresses through our union.

Key aspects of natural expression:

Effortless Flow: Like light naturally shining through a clean window, divine life naturally expresses through unhindered union. The Mirror Bible illuminates this in John 15:5: "Those who remain in me, and I in them, will produce much fruit."

Intuitive Response: Similar to how a skilled dancer naturally responds to music, union produces natural responses to life's situations. The Passion Translation captures this in Romans 8:14: "For all those who are led by the Spirit of God are sons of God."

Authentic Expression: Just as each snowflake uniquely expresses the same principles of crystallization, each person uniquely expresses divine life through their individuality. The Mirror Bible expresses this in Ephesians 2:10: "We are his poetry, created in Christ Jesus for good works."

Daily Life in Union

Consider how differently a tree experiences wind compared to a billboard. The billboard rigidly resists, while the tree flexibly flows with the wind through its deep connection to its roots. Similarly, daily life flows differently when lived from union rather than resistance. The Mirror Bible expresses this reality in Colossians 2:6-7: "As you have received Christ Jesus the Lord, so walk in Him, rooted and built up in Him."

Think about how your body naturally maintains countless functions without your conscious effort. Your heart beats, cells regenerate, and systems coordinate—all from their union with life itself. The Passion Translation illuminates this natural functioning in Acts 17:28: "For in him we live and move and have our being."

Let me share a story that captures this truth. A master chef was teaching his apprentice about cooking without recipes. The apprentice was anxious about getting everything exactly right. The master explained, "Recipes are training wheels. True cooking comes when you're so united with the ingredients that you know what they want to become. Each vegetable, each spice speaks to you—you just need to listen." This perfectly illustrates how daily life flows from union—not through following rules but through living from relationship.

The early church father Gregory of Nyssa described this as "eternal progress in God." Like a plant that naturally turns toward sunlight without being told, we naturally orient toward divine life through our union. The Mirror Bible captures this in 2 Corinthians 3:18: "We are being transformed into the same image from glory to glory."

Practical expressions in daily situations:

In Decision Making: Rather than weighing pros and cons externally, decisions flow from internal knowing. The Passion Translation renders John 16:13: "The Spirit of Truth... will guide you into all truth."

In Relationships: Instead of trying to manufacture love, love flows naturally from union. The Mirror Bible expresses this in 1 John 4:19: "We love because he first loved us."

In Work: Rather than striving to be productive, creativity flows from rest in union. The Passion Translation illuminates this in John 15:5: "Those who remain in me will produce much fruit."

In Challenges: Instead of fighting circumstances, we flow with divine life through them. The Mirror Bible captures this in Romans 8:37: "In all these things we are super conquerors through him who loved us!"

Think about how a skilled potter works with clay. At the highest level, there's such union between potter and clay that the piece seems to form itself. The early church fathers called this state "synergy"—where our activity and God's activity become indistinguishable because they flow from union.

Union Consciousness

In the depths of the ocean, fish don't think about being in water—they're so naturally conscious of their environment that they move effortlessly within it. This illustrates union consciousness—not constantly thinking about union but living naturally from it. The Mirror Bible expresses this reality in Acts 17:28: "In him we live and move and have our being."

Consider how a professional athlete maintains "zone consciousness." They're not thinking about being in the zone—they're so present in it that action flows naturally. The Passion Translation illuminates this state in Colossians 3:3: "Your secret life is now hidden in God as you are placed into the revelation of the life of Christ."

Let me share a story that captures this truth. A master calligrapher was asked about maintaining focus during complex pieces. He smiled and said, "I don't maintain focus—I maintain union. When I'm one with the brush, the ink, and the paper, focus happens naturally. It's not about concentration; it's about communion." This perfectly illustrates how union consciousness works—not through effort but through awareness of reality.

The early church father Gregory of Nyssa described this as "perpetual prayer"—not constant verbal prayer but continuous awareness of our life in God. The Mirror Bible captures this in 1

Thessalonians 5:17: "Pray without ceasing." This isn't about endless words but endless consciousness of union.

Think about how your body maintains balance. You don't consciously think about each muscle adjustment—there's a natural awareness that maintains equilibrium. The Passion Translation renders Philippians 2:13: "God himself is at work in you, inspiring you to want those things which please him."

Key aspects of union consciousness:

Natural Awareness: Like a bird's innate awareness of air currents, we develop natural consciousness of divine life. The Mirror Bible expresses this in Romans 8:16: "The Spirit himself bears witness with our spirit that we are children of God."

Present Reality: Similar to how fish don't strive to stay in water, we don't strive to maintain union—we awaken to its constant reality. The Passion Translation illuminates this in 2 Peter 1:3: "His divine power has given us everything we need for life and godliness."

Effortless Alignment: Just as a sunflower naturally turns toward the sun, our consciousness naturally aligns with divine life. The Mirror Bible captures this in 2 Corinthians 3:18: "We are transformed by the Spirit of the Lord in our constant beholding."

Living as One

Consider how light and its radiance are inseparable—the radiance doesn't strive to stay connected to light; it simply expresses light's nature. This illustrates living as one with divine life. The Mirror Bible expresses this reality in 1 John 4:17: "As he is, so are we in this world!"

Think about how a masterful pianist becomes one with the music. At the highest level, there's no separation between musician and music—they've become a single expression. The Passion

Translation captures this unity in Galatians 2:20: "And now the essence of this new life is no longer mine, for the Anointed One lives his life through me—we live in union as one!"

Let me share a story that illuminates this truth. A master glass artist was known for creating pieces that seemed alive with light. When asked his secret, he explained, "I stopped trying to make the glass do what I want and learned to become one with its nature. Now, each piece reveals what was always there—I just participate in its unveiling." This perfectly illustrates living as one—not imposing our will but expressing divine life naturally.

The early church father Maximus the Confessor described this as "becoming by grace what God is by nature." Like water taking on the properties of fire when heated, we don't lose our identity but express divine nature through our uniqueness. The Mirror Bible illuminates this in 2 Peter 1:4: "He has given us his very great and precious promises, so that through them you may participate in the divine nature."

Practical expressions of living as one:

Begin Each Day from Union: Like a tree naturally drawing life from its roots, start each day conscious of your life source. The Passion Translation renders Colossians 3:3: "Your secret life is now hidden in God."

Face Challenges from Oneness: Instead of meeting problems alone, let divine wisdom flow naturally through union. The Mirror Bible expresses this in 1 Corinthians 2:16: "We have the mind of Christ!"

Work from Rest: Similar to how a river effortlessly carries ships, let divine life carry your activities. The Passion Translation captures this in Matthew 11:28-30: "Come to me... and you will find rest for your souls."

Build Relationships from Fullness: Just as a full cup naturally overflows, let relationships flow from your union rather than need.

The Mirror Bible illuminates this in 1 John 4:19: "We love because he first loved us."

Think about how a skilled surfer becomes one with the wave. They're not fighting the water or trying to control it—they're so united with its movement that they become a visible expression of its power. Living as one means becoming a visible expression of invisible life.

Chapter Summary

Living from union isn't about maintaining connection with God—it's about awakening to the reality that we're already one spirit with Him. Like a branch naturally expressing the vine's life, we're called to live from union rather than toward it. This transforms everything from decision-making to relationships to handling challenges. When we understand that union is our natural state, not something to achieve, our whole approach to life shifts. Instead of striving to connect with God, we learn to rest in and express the connection that already exists. This awareness changes how we pray, how we face difficulties, and how we relate to others—everything flows from the consciousness of our inseparable oneness with Christ. Just as a wave is never separate from the ocean, we discover that our life is eternally bound up in His.

Reflection Questions

1. How might your daily life change if you lived consistently from union rather than toward it?

2. What areas of your life still operate from separation consciousness rather than union reality?

3. How could your relationships transform if you lived from fullness rather than need?

4. What practical steps can you take to maintain awareness of your union with divine life?

5. How might your response to challenges change if you faced them from union rather than separation?

Chapter 13
Unique Glory Expression

Individual Manifestation of Divine Life

In a pristine diamond, each facet reflects light uniquely while expressing the same brilliance. None of the facets compete; each one's distinct angle contributes to the diamond's overall glory. This natural phenomenon illustrates how we each uniquely express divine life. The Mirror Bible captures this reality in 2 Corinthians 3:18: "We all, with unveiled face, beholding as in a mirror the glory of the Lord, are being transformed into the same image from glory to glory."

Consider how different this is from religious conformity that tries to make everyone express God the same way. The Passion Translation illuminates our unique design in Ephesians 2:10: "We have become his poetry, a re-created people that will fulfill the destiny he has given each of us." We're not called to identical expression but to authentic manifestation of divine life through our uniqueness.

Think about how a master symphony conductor brings out each instrument's unique voice while maintaining perfect harmony. The early church father Irenaeus expressed this when he wrote, "The glory of God is man fully alive." This isn't about losing individuality in divine life but about finding our truest expression through it.

Hidden Glory Revealed

Just as every fingerprint, every voice, every snowflake is unique, each of us carries and expresses a distinct facet of divine glory. The Mirror Bible expresses this mystery in Colossians 1:27: 'God wanted everyone to know this rich and glorious secret inside you: Christ in you, the hope of glory!' Like the infinite variety in creation—from countless galaxies to unique planetary systems to distinct DNA patterns—we each manifest God's glory in unrepeatable ways.

The Passion Translation illuminates this in Ephesians 3:10: 'Through the church, the manifold wisdom of God should be made known.' The word 'manifold' here suggests multi-colored, multi-faceted, endlessly diverse expressions. Just as creation itself proclaims God's glory through infinite variety (Psalm 19:1), each son and daughter reveals a unique aspect of divine nature.

There are no clones in God's family. Consider how:
- Every star differs in glory (1 Corinthians 15:41)
- Every member has a distinct function (Romans 12:4-5)
- Every expression adds to the whole (Ephesians 4:16)

Like a grand symphony where each instrument contributes its unique voice to the whole, or a vast mosaic where each tile adds its distinct color to the complete picture, we each manifest glory in ways that no one else can."

Understanding Unique Design

In nature, no two snowflakes are identical, yet each one perfectly expresses the principles of crystallization. This remarkable phenomenon illustrates how divine life expresses itself through endless unique patterns while maintaining perfect unity. The Mirror Bible expresses this reality in 1 Corinthians 12:4-6: "There are diversities of gifts, but the same Spirit. There are differences of ministries, but the same Lord. And there are diversities of activities, but it is the same God who works all in all."

Consider how DNA works. The same four basic nucleotides combine in countless unique ways to express life through millions of distinct species. The Passion Translation illuminates this in Psalm 139:13-14: "You formed my innermost being, shaping my delicate inside and my intricate outside, and wove them all together in my mother's womb. I thank you, God, for making me so mysteriously complex!"

Let me share a story that captures this truth. A master potter was known for never making the same piece twice. When asked why, he explained, "The clay speaks to me differently each time. Each piece has its own song waiting to be heard. My job isn't to impose sameness but to listen for uniqueness." This perfectly illustrates how divine design works—not through replication but through endless unique expression.

The early church father Maximus the Confessor described this as "unity without uniformity." Like how white light refracts into countless colors through a prism, divine life expresses itself through infinite unique manifestations. The Mirror Bible captures this in Ephesians 3:10: "Through the church, the manifold wisdom of God should be made known."

Think about how an orchestra works. Each instrument maintains its unique voice while contributing to a greater harmony. The Passion Translation renders 1 Corinthians 12:18: "But God has carefully designed each member and placed it in the body to function as he desires."

Key aspects of unique design:

Divine Intent: Like an artist who deliberately varies each brushstroke, God intentionally designs each person uniquely. The Mirror Bible expresses this in Ephesians 2:10: "We are his poetry, created in Christ Jesus for good works."

Purpose in Particularity: Similar to how each organ in the body has a unique function, our distinctive traits serve divine purpose. The Passion Translation illuminates this in Romans 12:4-5: "Just as our bodies have many parts and each part has a special function, so it is with Christ's body."

Glory Through Distinction: Just as a stained glass window creates beauty through distinct colored pieces, we manifest glory through our differences. The Mirror Bible captures this in 1 Peter 4:10: "As each has received a gift, use it to serve one another, as good stewards of God's varied grace."

Glory Through Personality

Consider how light passes through stained glass windows in a cathedral. The same light shines through each piece uniquely, creating not just individual colors but an entire symphony of illumination. This illustrates how divine life expresses through our personalities. The Mirror Bible captures this reality in 2 Corinthians 4:7: "We have this treasure in earthen vessels, that the excellence of the power may be of God and not of us."

Think about how differently various musical instruments express the same melody. A violin brings forth delicate nuances, while a trumpet declares with boldness—yet both express the same music perfectly. The Passion Translation illuminates this in 1 Corinthians 12:4: "There are different kinds of spiritual gifts, but the same Spirit is the source of them all."

Let me share a story that captures this truth. A master gardener was known for growing an extraordinary variety of roses. When asked why he didn't focus on just the most popular varieties, he explained, "Each rose has its own way of expressing beauty. Some shout with bold colors, others whisper with subtle fragrance. The garden's glory isn't in sameness but in celebrating each flower's unique expression." This perfectly illustrates how our personalities become channels for divine expression.

The early church father Gregory of Nyssa described this as "infinite variation of the divine image." Like how a single theme in music can be expressed through countless variations without losing its essential nature, divine life expresses itself through infinite personality variations. The Mirror Bible expresses this in 1 Corinthians 15:41: "There is one glory of the sun, another glory of the moon, and another glory of the stars; for one star differs from another star in glory."

Key aspects of personality expression:

Natural Flow: Just as water naturally takes the shape of its container while remaining water, divine life naturally flows through our personality while remaining divine. The Passion Translation renders 2 Corinthians 3:18: "We can all draw close to him with the veil removed from our faces."

Authentic Voice: Similar to how each bird has its unique song that perfectly expresses bird nature, our personalities have unique ways of expressing divine nature. The Mirror Bible illuminates this in Psalm 139:14: "I am fearfully and wonderfully made."

Divine Amplification: Like how an amplifier doesn't change the music but makes it more audible, our personalities don't alter divine life but make it more visible. The Passion Translation captures this in John 17:22: "The glory that you have given me I have given to them."

Individual Manifestation

In quantum physics, there's a fascinating phenomenon where a single particle can exist in multiple states simultaneously until it manifests in a specific way through observation. Similarly, divine life contains infinite potential that manifests uniquely through each individual. The Mirror Bible expresses this reality in Ephesians 2:10: "We are his poetry, we are the words of his story."

Consider how differently athletes express excellence in sports. A gymnast manifests grace and precision, while a weightlifter displays power and strength—yet both perfectly express athletic excellence. The Passion Translation illuminates this in 1 Corinthians 12:6: "God works all these things in different ways in different people but it is the same God at work through all of us."

Let me share a story that captures this truth. A master chef was teaching his students about creating signature dishes. One student was trying to exactly copy the master's style. The chef said, "Stop trying to cook like me. Your hands, your taste, your instincts are unique. The same ingredients will speak differently through you. True mastery isn't in replication but in authentic expression." This perfectly illustrates how divine life seeks unique manifestation through each person.

The early church father Irenaeus described this as "the glory of God is man fully alive." Like how a prism doesn't create colors but reveals what's already in light, our individuality doesn't create divine life but reveals unique aspects of it. The Mirror Bible captures this in 2 Corinthians 3:18: "We are transfigured by the Spirit of the Lord in our constant beholding, from glory to glory."

Practical aspects of individual manifestation:

Natural Expression: Just as each tree produces fruit according to its kind, divine life naturally expresses through our unique design. The Passion Translation renders John 15:5: "As you live in union with me as your source, fruitfulness will stream from within you."

Personal Style: Similar to how handwriting is uniquely personal while following universal principles, our expression of divine life is distinctly our own. The Mirror Bible illuminates this in 1 Peter 4:10: "Each one should use whatever gift he has received to serve others."

Divine Creativity: Like how an artist might use different techniques to express the same vision, divine life finds creative expression through our individuality. The Passion Translation captures this in Genesis 1:27: "So God created man in his own image... male and female he created them."

Corporate Harmony

In a rainforest ecosystem, thousands of unique species work together to create a harmonious whole, each contributing distinctly while maintaining perfect balance. This natural wonder illustrates how individual expressions of divine life create corporate harmony. The Mirror Bible expresses this reality in 1 Corinthians 12:12: "For just as the body is one and has many members, and all the members of the body, though many, are one body, so it is with Christ."

Consider how a great jazz ensemble works. Each musician improvises freely while maintaining perfect harmony with the whole. The Passion Translation illuminates this in Ephesians 4:16: "He makes the whole body fit together perfectly. As each part does its own special work, it helps the other parts grow, so that the whole body is healthy and growing and full of love."

Let me share a story that captures this truth. A master weaver was creating a complex tapestry using threads of many colors. An apprentice asked why he didn't use just one color for simplicity. The weaver replied, "The beauty isn't in the individual threads but in their relationship to each other. Each color becomes more glorious through its connection to the others." This perfectly illustrates how corporate harmony enhances individual expression.

The early church father Maximus the Confessor described this as "unity in diversity." Like how different notes in a chord create harmony not through sameness but through relationship, divine life creates corporate harmony through diverse expressions. The Mirror Bible captures this in Romans 12:5: "In Christ we, though many, form one body, and each member belongs to all the others."

Key aspects of corporate harmony:

Mutual Enhancement: Just as different spices in a meal enhance each other's flavors, unique expressions of divine life enhance one another. The Passion Translation renders 1 Corinthians 12:21: "The eye cannot say to the hand, 'I don't need you!'"

Complementary Function: Similar to how organs in a body serve different functions while maintaining perfect unity, each person's unique expression serves the whole. The Mirror Bible illuminates this in Ephesians 4:7: "But to each one of us grace has been given as Christ apportioned it."

Synergistic Impact: Like how an orchestra creates music beyond what any individual instrument could produce, corporate harmony creates impact beyond individual capability. The Passion Translation expresses this in Ecclesiastes 4:12: "A cord of three strands is not quickly broken."

Living Your Glory

Think about how a diamond captures light. It doesn't strain to shine—it simply allows light to interact with its unique cut and clarity. Similarly, living your glory isn't about effort but about allowing divine life to express through your unique design. The Mirror Bible expresses this reality in 2 Corinthians 3:18: "We all, with unveiled face, beholding as in a mirror the glory of the Lord, are being transformed into the same image from glory to glory."

Consider how different artists approach the same sunset. One might use bold oils, another subtle watercolors—yet each captures authentic beauty. The Passion Translation illuminates this in Ephesians 2:10: "We have become his poetry, a re-created people that will fulfill the destiny he has given each of us."

Let me share a story that captures this truth. A master musician was teaching about authentic expression. A student was trying to imitate famous performers. The master said, "Stop trying to be a copy of someone else's masterpiece. You are an original, and the world is waiting for your unique song." This perfectly illustrates how living your glory means expressing your authentic design.

The early church father Gregory of Nyssa described this as "becoming what you are." Like how a flower naturally blooms according to its type, we're called to manifest the glory already within us. The Mirror Bible captures this in Colossians 1:27: "Christ in you, the hope of glory!"

Practical expressions of living your glory:

Natural Flow: Like a river finding its natural course, let divine life flow through your unique personality. The Passion Translation renders John 7:38: "Rivers of living water will flow from within them."

Authentic Expression: Instead of imitating others, express divine life through your distinctive design. The Mirror Bible illuminates this in 1 Peter 4:10: "As each has received a gift, use it to serve one another."

Rest-Based Manifestation: Similar to how a tree doesn't strain to produce fruit—it simply expresses its nature—let glory flow from rest rather than effort. The Passion Translation expresses this in Matthew 11:28-30: "Come to me... and you will find rest for your souls."

Think about how different instruments create harmony not by becoming like each other but by being perfectly themselves. Living your glory means being fully yourself in Christ.

Chapter Summary

Unique glory expression isn't about achieving something new but about manifesting what's already true. Like facets in a diamond, each person is designed to express divine life uniquely while contributing to corporate harmony. This isn't about performance but about authentic expression of who we are in Christ. Just as each snowflake reflects light distinctly yet perfectly, we each carry and express divine nature in our own way. Our personalities, gifts, and even seeming limitations become channels for glory when we understand they're part of our unique design. This diversity of expression creates a symphony of divine life, where our individual authenticity contributes to the fuller revelation of Christ in creation. Rather than conforming to a single pattern, we're free to be fully ourselves—the unique sons and daughters we were created to be.

Reflection Questions

1. What unique aspects of your personality might be channels for divine expression?

2. How could your natural gifts become more effective by flowing from rest rather than effort?

3. What areas of your life still try to copy others rather than express your authentic design?

4. How might your contribution to corporate harmony increase through being more fully yourself?

5. What practical steps can you take to live more authentically from your unique glory?

Chapter 14

Cosmic Restoration

Creation Awaits Sons

In the Amazon rainforest, scientists have discovered something remarkable. When a section of degraded forest is reconnected to healthy forest, restoration happens not just through human intervention but through the forest's own healing network. Trees share nutrients and information through underground fungal networks, literally restoring life to damaged areas. This natural phenomenon illustrates our role in cosmic restoration—we're meant to be connection points through which divine life flows to restore creation. The Mirror Bible expresses this reality in Romans 8:19: "All of creation stands on tiptoe waiting in eager expectation for the unveiling of the sons of God."

Consider how differently Jesus approached creation compared to religious ascetics who saw the material world as something to escape. He turned water into wine, multiplied bread and fish, and spoke of the kingdom as leaven permeating dough. The Passion Translation illuminates this creation-affirming perspective in Colossians 1:20: "Through him, God reconciled everything to himself... things on earth and things in heaven."

Think about how a master conductor doesn't just lead the orchestra but releases each instrument's full potential, creating harmony that transforms both musicians and audience. The early church father Maximus the Confessor captured this when he wrote, "Man is not meant to escape creation but to transfigure it." We're not called to abandon creation but to participate in its restoration.

Understanding Cosmic Purpose

When God told Adam to "subdue the earth" and have dominion over creation (Genesis 1:28), He wasn't appointing a tyrant but a gardener-king who would partner in creation's development. Like a master painter who invites an apprentice to help complete a masterpiece, God designed humans to be co-creators in cosmic restoration. The Mirror Bible expresses this reality in Romans 8:29: "Those God foreknew he also predestined to be conformed to the image of his Son, that he might be the firstborn among many brothers and sisters."

Consider how coral reefs work. These living structures not only house countless species but actually create environments where new life can flourish. The Passion Translation illuminates this creative purpose in Ephesians 2:10: "We have become his poetry, a re-created people that will fulfill the destiny he has given each of us, for we are joined to Jesus, the Anointed One."

Let me share a story that captures this truth. A master architect was designing a revolutionary building that would actually help heal its environment—purifying air, creating habitats, generating energy. When asked about this unusual approach, he explained, "We're not just meant to minimize our impact on creation—we're meant to actively participate in its flourishing. Every structure should make its environment more alive, not less." This perfectly illustrates our cosmic purpose as restorers.

The early church father Irenaeus described humans as those who would "make the cosmos a paradise." Like how a skilled gardener doesn't just maintain plants but helps them reach their full potential, we're called to help creation achieve its ultimate purpose. The Mirror Bible captures this in Colossians 1:16-17: "For in him all things were created... all things have been created through him and for him... and in him all things hold together."

Think about how differently indigenous peoples often approach land compared to industrial exploitation. They see themselves as caretakers in a living system rather than consumers of dead resources. The Passion Translation renders Genesis 2:15: "The LORD God placed the man in the Garden of Eden to tend and watch over it."

Key aspects of cosmic purpose:

Creative Partnership: Like how a symphony conductor doesn't make the music but releases its potential, we're called to partner in creation's unfolding. The Mirror Bible expresses this in 1 Corinthians 3:9: "For we are God's fellow workers."

Restoration Authority: Similar to how a master restorer brings ancient art back to life, we have authority to participate in creation's restoration. The Passion Translation illuminates this in Acts 3:21: "Heaven must receive him until the time comes for God to restore everything."

Glory Manifestation: Just as a prism doesn't create light but reveals its hidden colors, we're designed to manifest creation's hidden glory. The Mirror Bible captures this in Romans 8:19-21: "For the creation waits in eager expectation for the children of God to be revealed... in hope that the creation itself will be liberated from its bondage to decay."

Creation's Groaning

In the natural world, there's a phenomenon called "trophic cascades" where the presence or absence of a single species can transform entire ecosystems. When wolves were reintroduced to Yellowstone, they didn't just affect deer populations—they changed river patterns, increased biodiversity, and restored balance to the entire system. This illustrates how creation groans for the mature sons of God to take their place. The Mirror Bible expresses this reality in Romans 8:22-23: "We know that the whole creation has been groaning as in the pains of childbirth right up to the present time. Not only so, but we ourselves... groan inwardly as we wait eagerly for our adoption as sons."

Consider how a musical instrument responds differently to a novice versus a master musician. Under immature handling, it groans with discordant notes. But in the hands of a master, it sings its true song. The Passion Translation illuminates this in Colossians 1:20: "And by the blood of his cross, everything in heaven and earth is brought back to himself—back to its original intent, restored to innocence again!"

Let me share a story that captures this truth. A master vintner was teaching about wine-making in an ancient vineyard. He explained how the vines, though centuries old, still responded to human touch—either flourishing or withering based on the gardener's understanding. "These vines," he said, "know the difference between someone who sees them as mere crops and someone who understands their true nature. They're waiting for those who know how to call forth their highest expression." This perfectly illustrates how creation awaits sons who understand its true purpose.

The early church father Athanasius described creation as "pregnant with divine purpose." Like an unborn child moving in the womb, creation stirs with anticipation of its full manifestation through mature sons. The Mirror Bible captures this in Romans 8:19: "All of creation stands on tiptoe waiting in eager expectation for the unveiling of the sons of God."

Think about how different ecosystems respond to restoration when indigenous knowledge is applied versus industrial solutions. The land seems to recognize and respond to those who understand its deeper patterns. The Passion Translation renders Isaiah 55:12: "The mountains and hills will burst into song before you, and all the trees of the field will clap their hands."

Key aspects of creation's groaning:

Anticipatory Response: Like seeds that sprout at the right conditions, creation responds to authentic sonship. The Mirror

Bible expresses this in Mark 4:39: "Then He arose and rebuked the wind, and said to the sea, 'Peace, be still!'"

Resonant Recognition: Similar to how a tuning fork causes sympathetic vibrations in other instruments, creation recognizes and responds to mature sons. The Passion Translation illuminates this in Luke 19:40: "If they keep quiet, the stones will cry out."

Restored Purpose: Just as damaged DNA can be repaired by proper cellular function, creation awaits sons who can restore its original design. The Mirror Bible captures this in Acts 3:21: "Heaven must receive him until the time comes for God to restore everything."

Sons as Restorers

Consider how a master art restorer works. They don't impose their vision on the artwork—they reveal its original glory by removing what doesn't belong and strengthening what does. This illustrates how mature sons approach creation restoration. The Mirror Bible expresses this reality in Romans 8:21: "Creation itself will be liberated from its bondage to decay and brought into the freedom and glory of the children of God."

In ancient Japanese culture, there exists an art form called "kintsugi," where broken pottery is repaired with gold, making it more beautiful than before. This practice perfectly captures how mature sons don't just fix what's broken—they transform it into something more glorious. The Passion Translation illuminates this in 2 Corinthians 3:18: "We can all draw close to him with the veil removed from our faces. And with no veil we all become like mirrors who brightly reflect the glory of the Lord Jesus."

Let me share a story that captures this truth. A master permaculture designer was transforming a degraded landscape. Instead of fighting against existing patterns, she worked with them, turning problems into solutions. Where others saw weeds, she saw pioneer species preparing the soil. Where others saw erosion channels, she saw natural water patterns to enhance. "Our role," she explained, "isn't to dominate nature but to understand and enhance its inherent drive toward abundance." This perfectly illustrates how mature sons operate as restorers.

The early church father Maximus the Confessor described mature sons as "priests of creation." Like how a skilled mediator brings reconciliation by understanding both parties' true interests, mature sons understand both divine purpose and creation's patterns. The Mirror Bible captures this in Colossians 1:20: "Through him to reconcile to himself all things, whether things on earth or things in heaven."

Think about how differently Jesus approached nature compared to religious ascetics. He didn't withdraw from creation but engaged with it—turning water to wine, multiplying bread and fish, calming storms. The Passion Translation renders Mark 4:41: "Who is this man that even the wind and waves obey him?"

Key aspects of sons as restorers:

Understanding Purpose: Like a master architect who sees a building's original design beneath later modifications, mature sons see creation's true purpose. The Mirror Bible expresses this in Hebrews 11:3: "By faith we understand that the worlds were framed by the word of God."

Working with Nature: Similar to how a skilled surfer works with waves rather than against them, mature sons cooperate with creation's inherent patterns. The Passion Translation illuminates this in Matthew 6:28-29: "Look at the lilies of the field and how they grow."

Releasing Glory: Just as a master musician draws forth music already latent in the instrument, mature sons release creation's inherent glory. The Mirror Bible captures this in Psalm 19:1: "The heavens declare the glory of God."

The Scope of Restoration

Consider how even now we see glimpses of creation's response to mature sons. In talent shows worldwide, we witness how animals perform seemingly impossible feats under loving guidance—dogs solving complex problems, birds creating art, horses dancing in perfect rhythm. Even young children demonstrate extraordinary abilities when properly nurtured. These are but shadows of creation's potential awaiting the full manifestation of mature sons.

The Mirror Bible captures this progressive restoration in Isaiah 35:1-2: 'The wilderness and the wasteland shall be glad for them, and the desert shall rejoice and blossom as the rose.' This isn't mere poetic language—it's prophetic reality. We see this restoration expanding in concentric circles:

- Personal restoration (internal waste places becoming gardens of life)
- Environmental restoration (deserts blooming, waters flowing)
- Relational restoration (wolf dwelling with lamb, nations at peace)
- Cosmic restoration (black holes, dark matter, fallen angels)

Like Ezekiel's vision of living waters flowing from the temple (Ezekiel 47), life-giving restoration flows through mature sons into every realm of creation. The Passion Translation illuminates this in Romans 8:19-21: 'The creation waits in eager expectation for the children of God to be revealed... in hope that the creation itself will be liberated from its bondage to decay and brought into the freedom and glory of the children of God.'

This restoration isn't achieved through force but through revelation—as all creation discovers how good God really is. Like a master conductor drawing forth music that was always potential within the orchestra, mature sons release creation's true purpose and potential.

Manifesting Glory

In the physical world, there exists a phenomenon called "quantum entanglement," where particles become so connected that affecting one instantly affects the other, no matter the distance between them. This illustrates how mature sons are meant to be glory-activation points in creation. The Mirror Bible expresses this reality in 2 Corinthians 3:18: "We are being transformed into his likeness with ever-increasing glory."

Consider how a master photographer doesn't create beauty but reveals what's already present by understanding light, timing, and perspective. The Passion Translation illuminates this in Psalm 19:1-2: "The heavens declare the glory of God, and the sky above proclaims his handiwork. Day after day it pours forth speech."

Let me share a story that captures this truth. A master glassblower was known for creating pieces that seemed to capture light itself. When asked his secret, he explained, "I don't create the light—I create spaces for light to reveal its glory. The beauty was always there in the light; I just provide the lens for others to see it." This perfectly illustrates how mature sons manifest creation's hidden glory.

The early church father Gregory of Nyssa described this as "becoming transparent to glory." Like how a prism doesn't create colors but reveals the glory hidden in white light, mature sons reveal the glory hidden in creation. The Mirror Bible captures this in Romans 8:19: "For all creation awaits eagerly the unveiling of the sons of God."

Think about how differently Jesus manifested glory compared to religious leaders seeking to display their own importance. He revealed glory by serving, healing, and restoring—making visible the invisible life of God. The Passion Translation renders John 2:11: "This miraculous sign at Cana in Galilee was the first time Jesus revealed his glory. And his disciples believed in him."

Key aspects of manifesting glory:

Revealing Hidden Reality: Like an ultraviolet light revealing patterns invisible to natural sight, mature sons make visible what's hidden. The Mirror Bible expresses this in Colossians 1:27: "Christ in you, the hope of glory!"

Natural Expression: Similar to how a healthy tree naturally produces fruit, glory manifests naturally through aligned sons. The Passion Translation illuminates this in John 15:8: "When your lives bear abundant fruit, you demonstrate that you are my mature disciples."

Catalytic Presence: Just as a catalyst causes reactions by its mere presence, mature sons activate glory through who they are. The Mirror Bible captures this in 2 Corinthians 2:14: "But thanks be to God, who always leads us in triumph in Christ, and manifests through us the sweet aroma of His knowledge in every place."

Living Restoration Now

Consider how a seed contains not just its own future but the potential to transform an entire ecosystem. Similarly, mature sons carry restoration potential that affects everything around them. The Mirror Bible expresses this present reality in Colossians 1:27: "Christ in you, the hope of glory!"

Think about how differently a master gardener approaches a neglected garden compared to someone just trying to maintain it. Where others see weeds and chaos, the master gardener sees patterns and potential. The Passion Translation illuminates this in Isaiah 58:12: "You will be known as the Repairer of Broken Walls, Restorer of Streets with Dwellings."

Let me share a story that captures this truth. A master craftsman was teaching restoration principles to his apprentices. One apprentice was overwhelmed by a particularly damaged piece.

The master explained, "Don't focus on the damage—focus on the original design still present within it. Our job isn't to impose something new but to call forth what's already there." This perfectly illustrates how we live as restoration agents now.

The early church father Irenaeus described this as "practicing resurrection." Like how spring doesn't strive to overcome winter but naturally manifests new life, we manifest restoration through our union with Christ. The Mirror Bible captures this in 2 Corinthians 5:17: "Therefore, if anyone is in Christ, the new creation has come: The old has gone, the new is here!"

Practical expressions of living restoration:

Begin Each Day as a Restoration Point: Like how a healthy cell naturally affects its environment, let restoration flow from who you are. The Passion Translation renders Matthew 5:13-14: "You are the salt of the earth... You are the light of the world."

See with Restoration Eyes: Similar to how an artist sees the masterpiece in raw materials, view everything through the lens of its restored potential. The Mirror Bible expresses this in 2 Corinthians 5:16: "From now on we regard no one from a worldly point of view."

Work from Rest: Just as nature restores itself most powerfully when we align with its patterns rather than force them, let restoration flow from rest rather than striving. The Passion Translation illuminates this in Matthew 11:28-30: "Come to me... and you will find rest for your souls."

Think about how light transforms environments not through effort but through presence. The early church fathers saw this as a picture of how mature sons affect creation—not through striving but through being.

Chapter Summary

Cosmic restoration isn't just a future event—it's a present reality flowing through mature sons. Like a master restorer who sees and calls forth original design, we're called to participate in creation's transformation through our union with Christ. All creation eagerly awaits this revealing of mature sons who understand their role in divine restoration. As we live from our true identity, we naturally begin to impact the world around us—not through forced effort, but through the overflow of divine life within us. Just as a healthy tree naturally affects its entire ecosystem, our conscious union with Christ releases transformative life into every sphere we touch. This restoration extends beyond personal transformation to impact families, communities, culture, and even the physical creation itself, as we partner with God in bringing heaven's reality into earth's experience.

Reflection Questions

1. How might your environment change if you consistently lived as a restoration point?

2. What areas of creation around you are awaiting sons to reveal their glory?

3. How could your work become more effective by flowing from rest rather than effort?

4. What practical steps can you take to see with restoration eyes?

5. How might your impact increase by focusing on being rather than doing?

Chapter 15

Present-Tense Inheritance

Living from What's Already True

In quantum physics, there's a state called "quantum superposition" where a particle exists in all its possible states simultaneously until it's observed. Similarly, our inheritance in Christ isn't something waiting to happen—it's a present reality waiting to be observed and manifested. The Mirror Bible expresses this reality in Ephesians 1:3: "Blessed be the God and Father of our Lord Jesus Christ, who has blessed us with every spiritual blessing in the heavenly places in Christ."

Consider how differently a crown prince lives compared to someone hoping to achieve nobility. The prince doesn't work toward inheritance—he lives from it. The Passion Translation illuminates this in Romans 8:17: "And since we are his true children, we qualify to share all his treasures, for indeed, we are heirs of God himself. And since we are joined to Christ, we also inherit all that he is and all that he has."

Think about how a tree accesses resources. It doesn't strive to create nutrients and water—it simply draws from what's already present in its root system. The early church father Irenaeus captured this when he wrote, "The glory of God is man fully alive." We're not waiting for inheritance—we're learning to live from what's already ours.

Understanding Present Reality

Many believers have relegated inheritance to a future heaven, waiting for death to access what God has already given. This fundamentally misunderstands inheritance's nature. The Mirror Bible expresses this present reality in Ephesians 1:3: 'Blessed be the God and Father of our Lord Jesus Christ, who has blessed us with every spiritual blessing in the heavenly places in Christ.' Notice the tense—has blessed, not will bless.

Inheritance isn't triggered by our death but by Christ's death. Like a legal will that takes effect upon the testator's death, our inheritance was released through Christ's finished work. The Passion Translation illuminates this in Galatians 4:1-7: 'As long as an heir is underage, he is no different from a slave... But when the set time had fully come... you are no longer a slave, but God's child; and since you are his child, God has made you also an heir.'

This inheritance includes:
- Union and oneness with God
- Eternal and immortal life
- Complete wholeness
- Divine abundance
- Transfigured life

Like quantum physics where observation collapses wave functions into particle reality, mature sons bring heaven's invisible realities into earth's visible manifestation. This isn't about waiting for Jesus to return and restore all things—Acts 3:21 reveals that heaven must retain Him until we, the ekklesia, participate in this restoration. The Mirror Bible captures this in John 14:12: 'Whoever believes in me will do the works I have been doing, and they will do even greater things than these.'

This means:
- Operating like Jesus did—multiplying food, healing sickness
- Working with angels
- Releasing glory to creation's ends
- Impacting the entire cosmos
- Bringing invisible realities into visible manifestation

We don't have to live in lack—we've been given all things in Christ. Like a quantum leap that doesn't traverse the space between points but manifests instantly in the new position, we access inheritance through consciousness rather than process."

Consider a masterpiece in an art gallery. The lighting doesn't create the painting's beauty—it reveals what's already there. Similarly, our inheritance isn't something being created over time—it's a present reality being revealed. The Mirror Bible expresses this truth in 2 Peter 1:3: "His divine power has already given us everything we need for life and godliness through our knowledge of him."

Let me share a story that captures this truth. A wealthy father prepared an elaborate inheritance for his son, including businesses, properties, and resources. The son, though legally owner of everything, lived like a pauper because he didn't understand what was already his. One day, the father took him to the family vault and said, "Everything here has been yours since the day you were born. You haven't been waiting for inheritance—you've been living beneath it." This perfectly illustrates how many believers live beneath their present inheritance in Christ.

The Passion Translation illuminates this reality in Ephesians 1:3: "Every spiritual blessing in the heavenly realm has already been lavished upon us as a love gift from our wonderful heavenly Father, the Father of our Lord Jesus—all because he sees us wrapped into Christ."

Think about how differently a person approaches their own house versus a hotel room. In a hotel, they're careful not to move things or make changes. But in their own house, they live with full authority and access. The early church father Athanasius described this as "becoming by grace what God is by nature." We're not guests hoping to earn permanent residence—we're family members with full present access.

Consider how DNA works. A baby doesn't gradually receive their parents' genetic code—it's fully present from conception. The

Mirror Bible captures this in Colossians 2:9-10: "For in Christ all the fullness of Deity lives in bodily form, and in Christ you have been brought to fullness."

Key aspects of present reality:

Complete Provision: Like a fully furnished house waiting to be occupied, everything we need is already provided. The Passion Translation renders Philippians 4:19: "I am convinced that my God will fully satisfy every need you have, for I have seen the abundant riches of glory revealed to me through Jesus Christ!"

Present Access: Similar to how a key provides immediate access to a house, our union with Christ gives present access to all inheritance. The Mirror Bible expresses this in Hebrews 4:16: "Let us therefore come boldly to the throne of grace."

Full Authority: Just as an authorized signatory has immediate banking access, we have present authority in Christ. The Passion Translation illuminates this in Luke 10:19: "Now you understand that I have imparted to you my authority to trample over his kingdom. You will trample upon every demon before you and overcome every power Satan possesses."

Living from Fullness

Consider how an ocean deals with a drought—it doesn't worry about running dry because it lives from fullness rather than scarcity. Similarly, living from inheritance means operating from completeness rather than lack. The Mirror Bible expresses this reality in Colossians 2:10: "And in him you have been made complete, and he is the head over all rule and authority."

Let me share a story that captures this truth. A master musician was teaching about performance anxiety. A student was struggling with fear of making mistakes. The master explained, "Your fear comes from approaching the music from emptiness, trying to create something perfect. Instead, approach from fullness—the music is already complete within you. You're not creating it; you're releasing what's already there." This perfectly illustrates the difference between living toward inheritance and living from it.

The Passion Translation illuminates this in John 1:16: "From his fullness we have all received grace upon grace." Notice the language—we have received, not will receive. Living from fullness means operating from what's already true.

Think about how differently a wealthy person shops compared to someone in poverty. The wealthy person isn't constrained by whether they can afford something—they simply choose what best serves their purpose. The early church father Gregory of Nyssa described this as "movement according to nature." When we know our inheritance, we move naturally from abundance rather than striving from scarcity.

Key aspects of living from fullness:

Operating from Rest: Like a tree that produces fruit naturally because it's connected to its source, we live from connection rather than effort. The Mirror Bible expresses this in John 15:5: "I am the vine, you are the branches. Those who remain in me, and I in them, will produce much fruit."

Giving from Abundance: Similar to how a river naturally overflows because it's full, we give because we're full, not to become full. The Passion Translation captures this in 2 Corinthians 9:8: "God is able to make every blessing of his overflow into your lives."

Living from Position: Just as a royal heir naturally accesses palace resources, we access inheritance from our position in Christ. The Mirror Bible illuminates this in Ephesians 2:6: "And he raised us up with him and seated us with him in the heavenly places in Christ Jesus."

Manifesting Inheritance

In quantum physics, particles exist in multiple potential states until observed, at which point they manifest in specific ways. Similarly, our inheritance moves from potential to manifestation through conscious awareness. The Mirror Bible expresses this reality in 2 Corinthians 3:18: "We are transformed by the Spirit of the Lord in our constant beholding, from glory to glory."

Consider how a master photographer works with light. They don't create light—they position themselves and their subject to reveal what's already present. The Passion Translation illuminates this in Ephesians 5:13-14: "But when anything is exposed to the light, it becomes clear and visible... Christ will shine his light upon you."

Let me share a story that captures this truth. A master glassblower was teaching about creating complex pieces. A student was struggling, trying to force the glass into shape. The master said, "Stop trying to make something happen. Instead, become aware of what the glass wants to become. Your role isn't to create but to facilitate what's already potential within it." This perfectly illustrates how inheritance manifests—not through effort but through aligned awareness.

The early church father Gregory of Nyssa described this as "becoming what you are." Like how a seed doesn't strive to become a tree—it simply aligns with its nature—we manifest inheritance by aligning with our true identity. The Mirror Bible captures this in 1 John 4:17: "As he is, so are we in this world!"

Think about how differently water behaves at different temperatures. At 211 degrees, it's hot water. At 212 degrees, it transforms into steam with entirely new properties. Small shifts in awareness can similarly transform how inheritance manifests. The Passion Translation renders Romans 12:2: "Be inwardly transformed by the Holy Spirit through a total reformation of how you think."

Key aspects of manifesting inheritance:

Awareness Before Action: Like a dancer finding their center before moving, we manifest from consciousness rather than effort. The Mirror Bible expresses this in Colossians 3:1-2: "Since, then, you have been raised with Christ, set your hearts on things above."

Natural Expression: Similar to how a healthy body naturally expresses life, inheritance flows naturally through aligned consciousness. The Passion Translation illuminates this in John 7:38: "Rivers of living water will flow from within them."

Present Reality: Just as light doesn't become light—it is light—we don't become heirs; we manifest what we already are. The Mirror Bible captures this in Romans 8:17: "And if we are children, then we are heirs."

Kingdom Economics

In nature, there exists an economic system called "mycorrhizal networks" where trees share resources through underground fungal connections, operating from abundance rather than scarcity. This natural phenomenon illustrates kingdom economics. The Mirror Bible expresses this reality in 2 Corinthians 9:8: "And God is able to make all grace abound toward you, that you, always having all sufficiency in all things, may abound to every good work."

Consider how differently a wealthy family handles resources compared to those in poverty consciousness. The wealthy naturally invest, share, and multiply resources, while scarcity thinking focuses on preservation and protection. The Passion Translation illuminates this in Luke 6:38: "Give, and it will be given to you. A good measure, pressed down, shaken together and running over, will be poured into your lap."

Let me share a story that captures this truth. A master investor was teaching his protégé about wealth creation. The student was focused on saving and protecting capital. The master explained, "True wealth isn't about accumulation—it's about flow. Money is like blood in the body; its health is in its circulation, not its storage." This perfectly illustrates how kingdom economics operates on principles of flow rather than accumulation.

The early church father Basil the Great described this as "the bread in your cupboard belongs to the hungry." He understood that kingdom economics operates through distribution rather than hoarding. The Mirror Bible captures this in Acts 20:35: "It is more blessed to give than to receive."

Think about how a healthy ecosystem works. Nothing is wasted— everything flows in cycles of giving and receiving. The Passion Translation renders Philippians 4:19: "I am convinced that my God will fully satisfy every need you have, for I have seen the abundant riches of glory revealed to me through Jesus Christ!"

Key aspects of kingdom economics:

Flow Principle: Like a river that stays fresh through constant movement, kingdom resources multiply through circulation. The Mirror Bible expresses this in Luke 6:38: "Give, and it will be given to you."

Abundance Mindset: Similar to how a fruit tree produces far more seeds than needed for reproduction, kingdom economy operates from overflow. The Passion Translation illuminates this in John 10:10: "I have come to give you everything in abundance, more than you expect."

Supernatural Supply: Just as light doesn't diminish by being shared, kingdom resources multiply through distribution. The Mirror Bible captures this in 2 Corinthians 9:10: "He who supplies seed to the sower and bread for food will supply and multiply your seed for sowing."

Accessing Now

Consider how gravity works—you don't need to understand its principles or earn its effects to benefit from it. You simply need to align with it. Similarly, accessing inheritance isn't about qualification but alignment. The Mirror Bible expresses this reality in Colossians 2:10: "And you are complete in Him, who is the head of all principality and power."

Think about how differently you access resources in your own home versus someone else's house. In your home, you naturally access what you need without asking permission because you know it's yours. The Passion Translation illuminates this in Hebrews 4:16: "So now we come freely and boldly to where love is enthroned, to receive mercy's kiss and discover the grace we urgently need to strengthen us in our time of weakness."

Let me share a story that captures this truth. A master martial artist was teaching about accessing internal power. A student was straining to generate force. The master said, "Stop trying to create power—learn to access what's already there. True strength isn't generated; it's released." This perfectly illustrates how we access inheritance—not through striving but through awareness and alignment.

The early church father Maximus the Confessor described this as "natural movement according to nature." Like how a bird naturally accesses air currents, we learn to access inheritance through alignment with our true nature. The Mirror Bible captures this in 2 Peter 1:3: "His divine power has given us everything we need for life and godliness."

Practical steps for accessing now:

Begin Each Day from Fullness: Like waking up in your own house with full access to all resources, start each day conscious of your complete inheritance. The Passion Translation renders Ephesians

1:3: "Every spiritual blessing in the heavenly realm has already been lavished upon us."

Face Challenges from Abundance: Instead of reacting from lack, respond from the reality of full provision. The Mirror Bible expresses this in Philippians 4:19: "My God shall supply all your need according to His riches in glory."

Live from Position: Similar to how a prince naturally accesses royal resources, live from your position in Christ. The Passion Translation illuminates this in Romans 8:17: "And since we are his true children, we qualify to share all his treasures."

Think of how light naturally fills any space it's given access to. Your inheritance works the same way—it naturally manifests wherever awareness creates space for it.

Chapter Summary

Present-tense inheritance isn't something we achieve or earn—it's something we awaken to and align with. Like heirs learning to access what's already theirs, we're learning to live from fullness rather than striving toward it. This inheritance includes everything necessary for life and godliness, already deposited within us through our union with Christ. Just as a prince must learn to operate from his royal identity rather than earn it, we're discovering how to live from our position as sons and daughters who already possess all things in Christ. This shifts our entire approach to spiritual life—from pursuing what we think we lack to expressing what we already have, from working toward maturity to manifesting the fullness already within us. Through this consciousness of our inheritance, we naturally begin to access and demonstrate the divine resources, wisdom, and authority that have always been ours in Christ.

Reflection Questions

1. How might your daily life change if you consistently lived from inheritance rather than toward it?

2. What areas of your life still operate from scarcity rather than abundance consciousness?

3. How could your effectiveness increase by accessing inheritance through alignment rather than effort?

4. What practical steps can you take to maintain awareness of your complete inheritance?

5. How might your relationships transform if you lived consistently from fullness rather than need?

Chapter 16

The New Creation Race

Beyond First Adam

In nature, there are moments when an entirely new species emerges—not through gradual evolution but through sudden transformation. Scientists call these "quantum speciation events." This natural phenomenon illustrates what happened in Christ—not an improvement of human nature but the emergence of an entirely new creation. The Mirror Bible expresses this reality in 2 Corinthians 5:17: "Therefore, if anyone is in Christ, there is a new creation: everything old has passed away; look, everything has become new!"

Consider how different a butterfly is from a caterpillar. Though connected through metamorphosis, they are essentially different creatures with different capacities and natural habitats. The Passion Translation illuminates this transformation in Colossians 3:9-10: "For you have stripped away your old behavior with your old nature, and you have clothed yourselves with a brand-new nature that is continuously being renewed."

Think about how Jesus after His resurrection was both familiar and utterly different—able to eat fish yet pass through walls, recognizable yet transformed. The early church father Athanasius captured this when he wrote, "God became man so that man might become divine." This isn't about becoming something alien to our design but about manifesting our true nature in Christ.

Breaking Adam's Boundaries

In technology, there are moments when an innovation so fundamentally changes things that previous versions become obsolete—like how smartphones made traditional phones irrelevant. Similarly, Christ didn't just improve human nature; He inaugurated an entirely new species. The Mirror Bible expresses this reality in 1 Corinthians 15:45-47: "The first man Adam became a living being; the last Adam became a life-giving spirit... The first man was from the earth, earthy; the second man is from heaven."

Consider how different modern wheat is from its ancient wild ancestor. Though connected historically, they are fundamentally different in nature and capacity. The Passion Translation illuminates this transformation in Romans 5:17: "For if death dominated us through one man's failure, how much more will we continue to experience abundant life through the grace gift of righteousness given to us by the one man, Jesus, the Messiah!"

Let me share a story that captures this truth. A master geneticist was explaining to his students about breakthrough moments in species development. "Sometimes," he said, "a change is so fundamental that we can't even call it an improvement—it's an entirely new beginning. The butterfly doesn't fly better than the caterpillar; it belongs to an entirely different order of being." This perfectly illustrates our reality in Christ—not improved humans but an entirely new creation.

The early church father Irenaeus described this as "recapitulation"—Christ didn't just repair what Adam broke; He began something entirely new. Like how digital technology didn't just improve analog but created a new paradigm, Christ inaugurated a new species. The Mirror Bible captures this in Romans 8:29: "Those God foreknew he also predestined to be conformed to the image of his Son, that he might be the firstborn among many brothers and sisters."

Think about how differently a fish and an amphibian relate to water. The fish can only survive in water, while the amphibian can thrive in both water and land. The Passion Translation renders 1 Corinthians 15:49: "Just as we have borne the image of the earthly man, so shall we bear the image of the heavenly man."

Key aspects of moving beyond Adam:

Complete Transcendence: Like how a spacecraft breaks free from Earth's gravity into a new environment, we've moved beyond Adamic limitations. The Mirror Bible expresses this in 2 Corinthians 5:16: "From now on we regard no one from a worldly point of view."

New Operating System: Similar to how quantum computers operate on entirely different principles than classical computers, we function from new life rather than improved old life. The Passion Translation illuminates this in Galatians 2:20: "My old identity has been co-crucified with Messiah and no longer lives."

Different Source: Just as a solar-powered device draws energy from a different source than a battery-powered one, we live from Christ's life rather than Adam's. The Mirror Bible captures this in Colossians 3:3: "For you died, and your life is now hidden with Christ in God."

New Species Reality

In marine biology, there's a fascinating creature called the pistol shrimp that can create temperatures as hot as the sun's surface through a unique cavitation bubble. This unprecedented capability isn't an improvement of existing features—it's an entirely new order of function. Similarly, the new creation species operates with capabilities that transcend natural human capacity. The Mirror Bible expresses this reality in 1 John 4:17: "As he is, so are we in this world!"

Consider how different electricity is from mechanical power. While mechanical power improves through efficiency, electricity operates on entirely different principles. The Passion Translation illuminates this in 2 Peter 1:4: "As a result of this, he has given you magnificent promises that are beyond all price, so that through the power of these tremendous promises you can experience partnership with the divine nature."

Let me share a story that captures this truth. A master quantum physicist was explaining to students why quantum computers are different from classical ones. "We're not talking about faster calculations," he explained. "We're talking about a fundamentally different way of processing reality. What's impossible for classical computers isn't just easier for quantum computers—it's natural to them." This perfectly illustrates how the new creation species doesn't just do things better—it operates differently.

The early church father Gregory of Nyssa described this as "eternal progress in God." Like how a bird naturally operates in three dimensions while a land animal is limited to two, the new creation species naturally functions in spiritual dimensions. The Mirror Bible captures this in Ephesians 2:6: "And He raised us up together with Him and seated us together in the heavenly places in Christ Jesus."

Key aspects of new species reality:

Natural Supernatural: Like how a dolphin's sonar is supernatural to land mammals but natural to the species, spiritual capabilities are natural to the new creation. The Passion Translation renders John 14:12: "The person who believes in me will do the same works I have done, and even greater works."

Different Laws: Similar to how airplanes operate according to aerodynamic laws that seem to defy gravity, we operate according to spiritual laws that transcend natural limitations. The Mirror Bible expresses this in Romans 8:2: "For the law of the Spirit of life in Christ Jesus has made me free from the law of sin and death."

New Consciousness: Just as a butterfly naturally thinks in terms of flight while a caterpillar thinks in terms of crawling, we're meant to think from new creation reality. The Passion Translation illuminates this in 1 Corinthians 2:16: "But we possess the mind of Christ!"

Divine-Human Nature

In physics, light demonstrates a remarkable quality called "wave-particle duality"—being fully wave and fully particle simultaneously without contradiction. This natural phenomenon illustrates our divine-human nature in Christ. Like Jesus who was fully divine and fully human, we now participate in both natures. The Mirror Bible expresses this reality in 2 Peter 1:4: "Through these he has given us his very great and precious promises, so that through them you may participate in the divine nature."

Consider how grafted branches share both their original nature and the nature of their new root system. The Passion Translation illuminates this in John 15:5: "I am the sprouting vine and you're my branches. As you live in union with me as your source, fruitfulness will stream from within you."

Let me share a story that captures this truth. A master metallurgist was teaching about alloys. "When we combine gold and titanium," he explained, "we don't get something that's partly gold and partly titanium. We get a new material that fully expresses both natures simultaneously. It's not a compromise—it's a synergy." This perfectly illustrates how divine and human natures unite in the new creation.

The early church father Maximus the Confessor described this as "becoming by grace what God is by nature." Like how adopted children legally share both their birth heritage and their adoptive family's rights, we fully share both human and divine nature. The Mirror Bible captures this in 1 John 4:17: "As he is, so are we in this world!"

Think about how Jesus demonstrated this divine-human reality. He got hungry (human) yet multiplied bread (divine). He slept in the boat (human) yet commanded storms (divine). The Passion Translation renders Colossians 2:9-10: "For in him all the fullness of Deity lives in bodily form, and in Christ you have been brought to fullness."

Key aspects of divine-human nature:

Complete Integration: Like how water and wine mix to become one substance while maintaining both natures, our human and divine aspects fully integrate. The Mirror Bible expresses this in 1 Corinthians 6:17: "But the person who is joined to the Lord is one spirit with him."

Natural Expression: Similar to how a bilingual person naturally expresses both languages, we naturally express both human and divine capacities. The Passion Translation illuminates this in Galatians 2:20: "Christ lives his life through me."

Unified Operation: Just as the human brain seamlessly integrates logical and intuitive functions, our divine-human nature operates in perfect harmony. The Mirror Bible captures this in Colossians 3:3-4: "For you died, and your life is now hidden with Christ in God. When Christ, who is your life, appears, then you also will appear with him in glory."

Future Glory Manifesting

In quantum mechanics, there's a phenomenon called "quantum tunneling" where particles manifest in places they seemingly couldn't reach—as if future possibilities break into present reality. This illustrates how future glory manifests through the new creation now. The Mirror Bible expresses this reality in 2 Corinthians 3:18: "We are transformed by the Spirit of the Lord in our constant beholding, from glory to glory."

Consider how an oak tree exists fully in its acorn while progressively manifesting over time. The Passion Translation illuminates this in 1 John 3:2: "Beloved, we are God's children now, and what we will be has not yet appeared; but we know that when he appears we shall be like him, because we shall see him as he is."

Let me share a story that captures this truth. A master sculptor was working with a massive block of marble. A student asked why he kept stepping back to look at it. He explained, "I'm not just seeing what is—I'm seeing what's emerging. The masterpiece already exists in the marble; I'm participating in its manifestation." This perfectly illustrates how future glory progressively manifests through our awareness and alignment.

The early church father Gregory of Nyssa described this as "eternal progress." Like how a sunrise doesn't create light but progressively reveals what's already present, glory manifests through increasing awareness. The Mirror Bible captures this in Colossians 3:4: "When Christ who is our life appears, then you also will appear with Him in glory."

Think about how different frequencies of light reveal different aspects of reality. Ultraviolet light shows patterns invisible to natural sight, while infrared reveals heat signatures. The Passion Translation renders 2 Corinthians 4:17-18: "For our light and momentary troubles are achieving for us an eternal glory that far outweighs them all. So we fix our eyes not on what is seen, but on what is unseen."

Key aspects of future glory manifesting:

Progressive Revelation: Like dawn breaking gradually, glory manifests through increasing awareness. The Mirror Bible expresses this in 1 Corinthians 13:12: "For now we see in a mirror dimly, but then face to face."

Present Reality: Similar to how a hologram contains the whole image in each part, future glory is present now while continuing to manifest. The Passion Translation illuminates this in 1 John 4:17: "As he is, so are we in this world!"

Continuous Expansion: Just as the universe constantly expands, glory continues to manifest in increasing measure. The Mirror Bible captures this in Ephesians 3:20: "Now to Him who is able to do exceedingly abundantly above all that we ask or think, according to the power that works in us."

Living New Creation Now

Consider how electricity transforms a dark room. The power doesn't gradually build up—the moment the switch is flipped, darkness gives way to light. Similarly, living as new creation isn't about gradual improvement but about manifesting what's already true. The Mirror Bible expresses this reality in 2 Corinthians 5:17: "Therefore, if anyone is in Christ, the new creation has come: The old has gone, the new is here!"

Think about how differently an eagle moves compared to a chicken—not through effort but through awareness of its true nature. The Passion Translation illuminates this in Isaiah 40:31: "But those who wait upon the Lord will renew their strength; they will mount up with wings like eagles."

Let me share a story that captures this truth. A master martial artist was teaching advanced students about true power. One student was straining to demonstrate strength. The master said, "Stop trying to be powerful—recognize the power that's already within you. A lion doesn't try to roar; it roars because that's its nature." This perfectly illustrates living from new creation reality—not through effort but through awareness.

The early church father Athanasius described this as "becoming what we are." Like how a prince naturally carries royal authority not through striving but through awareness of identity, we live from new creation reality through consciousness of who we are. The Mirror Bible captures this in Romans 8:37: "In all these things we are more than conquerors through him who loved us."

Practical expressions of new creation living:

Natural Operation: Like how birds naturally fly without instruction manuals, let new creation life flow naturally through awareness. The Passion Translation renders Galatians 5:25: "If we live by the Spirit, let us also walk by the Spirit."

Present Reality: Similar to how light doesn't become light—it is light—live from what's already true rather than toward what could be. The Mirror Bible expresses this in Colossians 2:10: "And you are complete in Him."

Glory Expression: Just as a diamond naturally reflects light according to its design, let glory manifest through your unique design. The Passion Translation illuminates this in 2 Corinthians 3:18: "We are being transformed into his image with ever-increasing glory."

Chapter Summary

The new creation race isn't about improving human nature but about manifesting an entirely new species reality in Christ. Like quantum transformation rather than gradual evolution, we've moved beyond first Adam into a divine-human nature that naturally expresses future glory now. This isn't about becoming better versions of ourselves but about awakening to an entirely new order of being—one that transcends the limitations of fallen humanity. Just as a butterfly emerges as a completely new creature rather than a better caterpillar, we've been transformed into a new species that naturally carries and expresses divine life. This new creation reality means we're not bound by the genetic or spiritual limitations of the first Adam but are free to manifest the capacities and qualities of the Last Adam, Christ Himself. We're not evolving toward divinity; we're awakening to the divine-human nature already established in us through our union with Christ.

Reflection Questions

1. How might your daily life change if you consistently lived from new creation reality rather than trying to improve old patterns?

2. What areas of your life still operate from old creation consciousness rather than new species reality?

3. How could your effectiveness increase by living from what's already true rather than striving toward what could be?

4. What practical steps can you take to maintain awareness of your divine-human nature?

5. How might your impact expand by living naturally from new creation reality?

www.ingramcontent.com/pod-product-compliance
Lightning Source LLC
Chambersburg PA
CBHW031039160726
47991CB00005B/1948